Y0-BDI-533

Edinburgh

Footprint

Alan Murphy

Contents

Footprint

Current titles:
Barbados
Berlin
Bilbao
Bologna
Cape Town
Copenhagen
Dublin
Havana
Madrid
Naples
Paris
Reykjavík
Sydney
Vancouver

Forthcoming titles:
Hong Kong
Lisbon
Marrakech
Seville
Turin
Verona

Footprint Handbooks
6 Riverside Court,
Lower Bristol Road,
Bath BA2 3DZ, UK
T +44 (0)1225 469141
F +44 (0)1225 469461

90 Footprint travel guides
to over 145 of the world's
most exciting countries
and cities in Latin America,
the Caribbean, Africa,
Indian sub-continent,
Australasia, Southeast Asia,
the Middle East, Europe,
North America.

www.footprintbooks.com

Edinburgh

Footprint

Alan Murphy

Listings

About the author

Alan Murphy's first attempts at busking at the Edinburgh Festival in 1985 may have put paid to any lingering hopes of a career as a jazz musician, but it was also the beginning of a beautiful friendship with the city. Following a spell in journalism in his native Scotland, Alan swapped shorthand notebook for rucksack and joined the Gringo Trail in South America. However, it was the writing bug that bit and he ended up working as a journalist in Bolivia. Since returning to Scotland he has written Footprint guides to Bolivia, Peru, Ecuador, Venezuela, Scotland, Scotland Highlands and Islands, Glasgow and Edinburgh, as well as contributing to several national newspapers and travel magazines. He now lives in Somerset with his wife and daughter.

Acknowledgements

Alan would like to thank all those who contributed to the book: John Binnie for researching and writing the Gay and lesbian section; John Murphy for researching and writing the Bars and clubs section; Duncan Lindsay for the Arts and entertainment section; and Frank Nicholas for Books. Thanks to everyone at the EdinburghTourist Board and the Fringe office for their valuable input, to the staff at the National Library of Scotland for their knowledge and to the hundreds of hoteliers, B&B owners, restauranteurs and bar staff for their enormous patience and good humour. Thanks also to Rebecca Ford, who made such a significant contribution to the Edinburgh section of the Scotland Handbook, and a big shout to everyone at Footprint, especially Catherine and Lambchop. As always, a huge amount of gratitude is owed to Philippa for her unbending love and support, and for keeping me laughing, and to Rosa, for helping to keep things in perspective.

Few cities make such a strong impression as Edinburgh. Dubbed the 'Athens of North', Scotland's ancient capital is undeniably beautiful, with a grandeur to match Paris or Prague, Vienna or Rome. There is the medieval Old Town with its labyrinth of soaring tenements and dark, sinister alleyways; the Georgian New Town with its genteel grey façades and wide, airy streets; and dominating everything, the brooding presence of the Castle.

Fittingly, such a setting provides the stage for the Edinburgh International Festival and its various offshoots, which together comprise the biggest arts event on the planet. But Edinburgh is more than just the sum of its arts. Its Hogmanay party is the biggest celebration in the northern hemisphere, and the arrival of the new Scottish Parliament has brought confidence and vitality to a city that was always thought of as being rather straight-laced. Edinburgh, once the most puritanical of places, has learned how to have fun, how to be stylish, and, heaven forbid, even how to be just a wee bit ostentatious.

Tattoo and Trainspotting

Edinburgh may be the most beautiful of Britain's cities, but it is also the most divided: half Tattoo half *Trainspotting*. Surrounding the wealth and elegance of the city centre is a ring of outlying estates containing areas of grinding poverty and festering alienation, populated by real-life characters from an Irvine Welsh novel. This is the Edinburgh the tourists don't see. The kind described by Ian Rankin in his best-selling Inspector Rebus novels, where drug addiction, violence and corruption are a part of everyday life, going on under the noses of cultural and political elites, and where radical counter-culturists rub shoulders with the prim and proper ladies of Morningside, the embodiment of Scottish puritanism.

Jekyll and Hyde city

There have always been two sides to Edinburgh, perhaps not surprisingly. For this is the city that inspired Robert Louis Stevenson's *Dr Jekyll and Mr Hyde*. In medieval times wealthy merchants and professionals lived cheek by jowl with the great unwashed in the cramped conditions of the Royal Mile. This uneasy social integration was brought to an end when those who could afford to decanted to the New Town, leaving the Old Town to degenerate into a decaying slum. The Old Town has since been cleaned up and is now the hub of Edinburgh's tourist activities. The slums are still there, however, only they've moved out to the fringes of the city, creating an even sharper social division. This is at its most evident in Leith, Edinburgh's old port, which has been tarted up with converted waterside apartments, fashionable bars and bistros and expensive restaurants. Only yards from such indulgence are grim, faceless council blocks, where single-parent families have to exist for a week on less than what you'd pay for a decent bottle of Chablis. It should be a recipe for revolution, but a healthy wit somehow seems to keep it all together.

At a glance

Old Town

The city centre is divided in two. South of Princes Street Gardens is the medieval Old Town, a rabbit warren of narrow alleys and closes. Running through the heart of the Old Town, from the Castle down to the Palace of Holyroodhouse, is the Royal Mile, one of the busiest tourist thoroughfares in the world. South of the Royal Mile the semi-subterranean Cowgate runs under the bridges to meet the cobbled Grassmarket, lined with rowdy boozers, and the upward sweep of Victoria Street with its quirky independent shops. South of the Royal Mile is also Edinburgh's Museumland, featuring the big two, the Museum of Scotland and Royal Museum of Scotland, as well as a few more ghoulish surprises, sprinkled amongst the older parts of the University. East of the Cowgate, Holyrood Road leads to the new Scottish Parliament building, due for completion late in 2003 and already attracting a growing number of hotels and restaurants which reflect the area's new-found cachet.

Arthur's Seat and Duddingston

Overlooking the parliament building is Edinburgh's largest volcano, Arthur's Seat, an authentic piece of mountain wilderness within a stone's throw of the city centre. Tucked behind Arthur's Seat is Duddingston, one of the city's few remaining urban villages.

New Town

North of Princes Street is the neoclassical New Town, built in the late 18th and early 19th centuries to improve conditions in the city. The main thoroughfare is George Street, which links St Andrew Square in the east and Charlotte Square in the west. Once the bastion of prudent financial management, this part of the New Town is now where the city's fashionistas like to spend their cash in style, though Charlotte Square has kept its serious business head.

Parallel to George Street is Princes Street, once the city's finest shopping street but now usurped by its trendy neighbour and looking a bit dowdy by comparison. North of George Street, Queen Street marks the boundary of the 'First New Town', as it was known, before it spread towards the Forth and multiplied.

Calton Hill and Broughton

The eastern New Town is bordered by Broughton Street, heart of the city's gay scene and one side of the so-called 'Pink Triangle'. As well as being home to many of the hippest bars and clubs this part of town has a laid-back feel, redolent of Manhattan's East Village. Looming over the Pink Triangle is Calton Hill whose summit and sides are studded with some of Edinburgh's most sublime Regency terraces as well as some of its most bizarre monuments.

Stockbridge and Inverleith

Only a ten-minute walk north from George Street is Stockbridge. Not that many visitors discover this former village, as the locals tend to keep it to themselves, but its nooks are worth seeking out. The streets have a real community feel – greengrocers' shops mingle with delis and bistros, jewellers and junk shops and second-hand bookstores – and the Water of Leith gently tickles its midriff. The neighbourhood rubs shoulders with Inverleith, altogether more suburban and sedate, but hiding the Royal Botanic Garden up its verdant sleeve.

West Edinburgh

The city's West End is a seamless extension of the New Town, with its perfect neoclassical symmetry and discreet old money. A short distance to the south, and possibly too close for comfort, is The Exchange, Edinburgh's shiny new international financial centre, which has breathed new life back into an area that had largely lain dormant since the demise of canal transport and the city's brewing industry. Incongruously placed on the other side of Lothian Road is Edinburgh's mini-theatreland, with a trio of the city's top arts venues supporting a cluster of good restaurants.

South Edinburgh

South Edinburgh is where town and gown meet head on. South from the Old Town is the district of Southside which today forms the heart of the University quarter. Only a stone's throw away, net curtains twitch at the antics of the city's undergraduates in the genteel suburbs of Bruntsfield, Merchiston and Morningside.

Leith, Newhaven and Portobello

Northeast of the city centre is Leith, Scotland's major port in its heyday, but when the fishing and shipping trade decanted south, the heart was ripped out of the district. Leith has undergone a dramatic transformation, however. Warehouse conversions, gourmet restaurants, bars and bistros line the waterside and the Royal Yacht Britannia sits proudly at her new home, Ocean Terminal. Flanking the rejuvenated old port, like a couple of antique bookends, are the sleepy former fishing port of Newhaven and the faded seaside resort of Portobello.

Around Edinburgh

Beyond the city bypass are the Lothians. East Lothian keeps an air of gentle well-being with its tidy rural towns and villages and string of exclusive golf courses, while neighbouring Midlothian is still struggling to recover from the devastation of the mining industry. West Lothian is home to Scotland's so-called 'Silicon Glen'. The region's high-tech industries were once held up as the bright pilot light to spark Scotland's economic recovery, but more recently the lustre has begun to fade with a series of closures.

Best

★ Ten of the best

1 **Museum of Scotland** Superb state-of-the-art building with innovative displays that take the mystery out of Scottish history, p60.

2 **Royal Yacht Britannia** Gain a real insight into royal life aboard the Windsors' favourite nautical residence, p100.

3 **Arthur's Seat** A huge dollop of genuine wilderness standing improbably in the middle of the city, p67.

4 **Scottish National Gallery of Modern Art** Worth visiting even if you know nada about Dada, its Terrace Café is divine on a sunny day, p88.

5 **Water of Leith Walkway** Bucolic bliss within earshot of the city centre traffic, ending at Leith Shore, where you can enjoy an al fresco drink on a summer's evening, p90.

6 **Edinburgh Castle** The city's great icon is unavoidable and it would be rude not to pay it a visit, p33.

7 **Ghost tour** Be afraid…be very afraid when you sign up for a nocturnal tour of the of the city that put the Mac into macabre, p28.

8 **Royal Botanic Garden** If the sun is shining do yourself a big favour and buy a load of goodies from Valvona & Crolla and come here for a picnic, p85.

9 **Rosslyn Chapel** The most mysterious church in the country is only seven miles from the city centre and home to more secrets and legends than an entire series of Harry Potter, p111.

10 **Edinburgh Festival** The best opera, classical, ballet and theatre, the newest films, the funniest comedians and thousands of people doing very strange things, there's nothing like it anywhere else on the planet, p198.

The ★ symbol in the book is used to indicate recommended sights.

Trip planner

Generally speaking, May to September are the warmest and driest months, with an average summer high of around 18-19°C, though you can expect rain at any time of the year. This is when Edinburgh receives the vast majority of visitors, particularly during the Festival, a cultural maelstrom held over four exhausting weeks during August and September. Finding accommodation anywhere near the centre of town is well nigh impossible at this time, so it's best to book up well in advance. Prices will also be higher. Another busy time is Hogmanay (New Year), though the freezing winter temperatures may leave you rueing the decision to wear your kilt native-style.

A day

This is by no means a definitive list but would make an enjoyable and varied day for those who have already visited the more obvious tourist sights. Start the day at the excellent Museum of Scotland, in Chambers Street, after which you'll have earned a much-needed coffee break at the Elephant House, on George IV Bridge. Then head down towards Princes Street and pop into the National Gallery of Scotland, which holds the city's finest collection of old masters. If you're feeling peckish, take a wee stroll down to Black Bo's on Blackfriars Street for a superb vegetarian lunch. Back down to Princes Steet for a bus to Ocean Terminal, home of the Royal Yacht Britannia, a real treat for monarchists and republicans alike. Then it's along to The Shore in Leith for a superb seafood dinner at Fishers, one of many classy eateries around this area.

A weekend

The city's greatest attraction is its looks. First up, get yourself to the top of Calton Hill, giving you the perfect opportunity to find your bearings, as well as to enjoy some fantastic views and to realise that Edinburgh is a small city and everything you need is within easy walking distance. If you're feeling energetic head down to the Palace of Holyroodhouse for a peek at the groovy new Scottish Parliament building, still under construction at time of going to press. From here, there are several options. You can take a tour round the palace, visit Dynamic Earth, one of Edinburgh's most successful new attractions, or take a walk up Arthur's Seat, a real, *bona fide* mountain wilderness right in the heart of the city. For something a little less strenuous explore the Water of Leith Walkway, which winds its bucolic way from the west of the city to Leith. Along the way you can make a few cultural diversions by popping in to the Scottish National Gallery of Modern Art and the Dean Gallery, on opposite sides of Belford Road. Further east, the Water of Leith passes close by the Royal Botanic Garden, surely worth an hour or two of anyone's time.

A long weekend
There are, of course, a thousand other things to do in this fine city. There's the small matter of Edinburgh Castle, from where the Royal Mile – 1,984 cobbled yards of dark, sinister history – leads downhill to the Palace of Holyroodhouse. And then there's all that wonderful architecture. You could spend a few days just wandering round the New Town ogling all those gorgeous neoclassical buildings. Start in Charlotte Square and head north into the splendour of Moray Place for a taste of what's on offer.

A week
A week would also allow you to venture beyond the city's generous limits to comb the beaches of East Lothian, walk in the wilds of the Pentland Hills, delve into the mysteries of Rosslyn Chapel, visit the magnificent Hopetoun House, or marvel at the Forth Rail Bridge from the vantage points of South or North Queensferry.

! Edinburgh's climate is notoriously fickle, hence the old saying that if you don't like the weather, then wait 20 minutes.

Contemporary Edinburgh

Edinburgh may be at least a thousand years old but it has only just come of age. Visit the city today and you'll find flourishing theatres, hip clubs, innovative museums, chic cafés and buzzy restaurants serving everything from tikka to tagine. Yet for years Edinburgh seemed as dormant as the volcanoes on which it was built. This was a city that was so beautiful, so full of history, that it didn't need to do anything to attract visitors: people came here anyway. It was a sedate place: a white collar city with a business life dominated by the legal and financial sectors. The only time of year it woke up was during the Festival – and it would quickly go back into hibernation as soon as the performers had packed up and gone home. The city had a reputation for being aloof and rather dull – and it really didn't care.

The reasons for this are partly historical, partly geographical. Although it had been the capital since the 12th century, Edinburgh had not necessarily been at the heart of Scottish life. Scotland's kings were always crowned at Scone Palace near Perth and, after the Union of the Crowns in 1603, preferred to spend their time in London anyway. Added to that was the fact that the city did not have a long tradition as the established seat of government. The old Scottish Parliament used to meet at locations throughout Scotland and did not make Edinburgh its permanent home until the 17th century. Only 70-odd years later, Scotland was united with England and government moved to Westminster.

The city's location was also a factor. Unlike most capital cities in the world, Edinburgh does not have a river running through its heart – and rivers do not just bring trade but energy and a cosmopolitan bustle. Encircled by the Pentland Hills and the chilly waters of the Firth of Forth, and dominated by its lofty Castle, the city seemed somehow trapped in splendid isolation – an impression heightened by its proximity to Glasgow, a warm, lively, industrial city that knew how to enjoy itself. In fact for many years Edinburgh

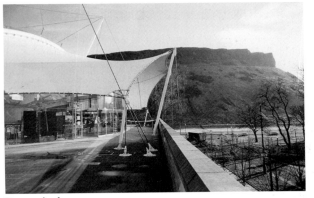

Dynamic duo
State-of-the-art geology lesson, Dynamic Earth, sits in the shadow of Salisbury Crags, inspiration for the theory of modern geology.

appeared to have been eclipsed by its great rival. Glasgow had worked hard to improve its image and by the late 1980s had gained a reputation for innovative arts and great shops and restaurants. It was a youthful city and Edinburgh seemed tired and middle aged in comparison. But Edinburgh fought back and during the 1990s a more vibrant culture began to emerge. Cappuccino and croissants replaced weak tea and scones as continental-style cafés and bistros opened, their tables spilling on to once-empty pavements in friendly gaggles. New attractions opened, such as the techno- tastic Museum of Scotland and Dynamic Earth. The former Royal Yacht Britannia found a permanent home in Leith docks and now attracts thousands of visitors each year. And venerable George Street, formerly the heart of the city's prudent financial sector, began to fill with fashionable bars and restaurants and designer stores.

Then, in 1997, Scotland voted for devolution and Edinburgh was chosen as the home for the new parliament. The city seemed to blossom overnight. It became a proper capital, a city at the very centre of Scottish life. There was a new confidence in the air and a fresh sense of purpose. Opposite Holyrood Palace work began on a bold new parliament building and, though the construction has been plagued by delay and controversy, with costs spiralling to well over £300 mn, it is hoped that the new MSPs (Members of the Scottish Parliament) voted in after the May elections won't have to wait too long before they move into their new home.

Today Edinburgh is rated the most desirable city in Britain in which to live and its population is growing fast. The restaurants and bars are busy; the clubs full of cool young things. Bold new buildings, like the award-winning Dancebase in the Grassmarket, have appeared, providing a refreshing change from all that gloomy medieval granite, and while there are still shops selling sensible skirts and twin sets, they have been joined by fashionista favourites such as Escada and Harvey Nichols.

The Festival is still the main event in the city's calendar. In August everyone who is anyone in the arts world heads north to Edinburgh. But the city no longer goes to sleep as soon as it is over. Then in December it's party time again, when Edinburgh hosts the biggest Hogmanay party in the world. A glittering giant wheel rotates next to the gothic splendour of the Scott Monument; Princes Street Gardens is transformed into an outdoor ice rink, and thousands of people sing and dance in Princes Street.

Edinburgh is now more confident, more fun, than ever before, and tries much harder to please. But it will always be a conservative city at heart – where people don't like to draw attention to themselves. It is still a city where flash is frowned upon, and where elderly ladies in hats think decadence is having two slices of shortbread with their afternoon tea. And while new buildings may be springing up everywhere, the alleyways of the Old Town are as atmospheric as ever, the broad streets of the New Town as elegant. Edinburgh may have changed – but not too much. It is still the most beautiful city in Britain – and it knows it.

The cheapest and quickest route to Edinburgh from Ireland and Europe is by plane. From England the cheapest way north is by coach: the London to Edinburgh journey takes around eight hours, and from Newcastle it's 1½ hours. There are fast and frequent rail services from London's King's Cross and regional cities in England to Edinburgh Waverley. Journey time from London is only about 4½ hours, but this can be a relatively expensive way to travel and, though there are various cheap offers available, these need to be booked well in advance.

Getting around Edinburgh is straightforward. This is a city on a human scale and most of what you'll want to see lies within the compact centre which is easily explored on foot. However, Edinburgh is also a hilly city and a full day's sightseeing can leave you exhausted. An excellent way to see the sights and avoid wearing out shoe leather is to take one of the city bus tours, which allow you to hop on and off any bus at any time.

Getting there

Air

There are daily direct flights to Edinburgh from all London airports, as well as from provincial UK airports, Ireland and several European capitals. There are no direct flights from North America; these are routed via London or Dublin, or you can fly to Glasgow. Fares are highest from around early June to mid-September, which is the tourist high season, and drop in the months either side of the peak season – mid-September to early November and mid-April to early June. They are cheapest in the low season, from November to April. The exception is during Christmas and New Year when seats are at a premium and prices rise sharply. It's also worth noting that flying at the weekend is normally more expensive. There are a number of low-cost airlines which regularly offer very cheap flights (from £10 one way from London), but check the hidden surcharges before booking. They are also subject to rigid restrictions and need to be booked well in advance.

From the UK and Ireland Aer Arran fly from Cork. **Aer Lingus** from Dublin. **BMI** from East Midlands, Leeds/Bradford and Manchester. **British Airways** from Belfast City and International, Birmingham, Bristol, Cardiff, Inverness, Jersey, Kirkwall, London Gatwick and Heathrow, Manchester, Shetland, Southampton, Stornoway and Wick. **British European** from Birmingham, Guernsey and Jersey. **easyjet/Go** from Bristol, London Gatwick, Luton and Stansted. **Eastern Airways** from Humberside and Norwich. **Euromanx** from Isle of Man. **Ryanair** from Dublin. **ScotAirways** from London City.

From Continental Europe Air France fly from Paris (Charles de Gaulle). **British Airways** from Paris (CDG) and Zurich. **KLMuk** from Amsterdam. **BMI** from Brussels and Copenhagen. **Lufthansa** from Frankfurt.

Airlines and agents

Aer Arran, **T** 0800-5872324, www.skyroad.com
Aer Lingus, **T** 0845-0844444, www.aerlingus.com
Air France, **T** 0845-0845444, www.airfrance.com
BMI, **T** 0870-6070555, www.flybmi.com
British Airways, **T** 0845-7733377, www.britishairways.com
British European, **T** 0870-5676676, www.flybe.com
easyJet/Go, **T** 0870-6000000, www.easyjet.com
Eastern Airways, **T** 01652-680600, www.easternairways.com
Euromanx, **T** 0870-1660102, wwweuromanx.com
KLMuk, **T** 0870-5074074, www.klm.com
Lufthansa, **T** 0845-7737747, www.lufthansa.com
Ryanair, **T** 0871-2460016, www.ryanair.com
Scot Airways, **T** 0870-6060707, www.scotairways.co.uk
All phone numbers listed above are in the UK.

Other websites
www.expedia.com
www.travelocity.com
www.lastminute.com
www.ebookers.com
www.opodo.com
www.cheapflights.com

Airport information Edinburgh international airport, **T** 333 1000 (general enquiries), **T** 344 3136 (airport information), is eight miles west of the city centre. Terminal facilities include a tourist information desk, Bureau de Change, ATMs, restaurants and bars (first floor) and shops (ground floor and first floor). The tourist information desk is located in the international arrivals area, and will book accommodation and car hire. The main international car hire companies are located in the terminal in the main UK arrivals area (see also p226). The airport is easily reached by car, just off the

➡ Travel extras

Safety Edinburgh is a reasonably safe place, but some areas are best avoided at night. Lothian Road and the Grassmarket are not particularly dangerous but full of beer-soaked revellers who may prove irritating. The Meadows' walkways are lonely at night and potentially risky, as are the narrow, secluded wynds and closes of the High Street. The back streets of Leith are also best avoided.

Money Edinburgh needn't be an expensive city to visit. Cheap accommodation is available in hostels or B&Bs and transport is relatively cheap. You can get by on £25-30 per day if you eat in cafés and pubs or cheap restaurants. Also most of the museums and galleries are free. If you want to enjoy the city's better restaurants and go out at night, you'll need at least £60-70 per day, without being extravagant. During the Festival you could easily add another £20-30 on top of that.

Telephone code Dial 0131 for Edinburgh from outside the city.

Time Greenwich Mean Time (GMT) is used from late October to late March, after which the clocks go forward an hour to British Summer Time (BST). GMT is five hours ahead of US Eastern Standard Time and 10 hours behind Australian Eastern Standard Time.

Tipping In a restaurant you should leave a tip of 10-15% if you are satisfied with the service. If the bill already includes a service charge, you needn't add a further tip. Tipping is not normal in pubs or bars. Taxi drivers will expect a tip for longer journeys; usually of around 10%.

A8. Car parking costs £1.70 per hour short term, or £4.70 per day long term. There is an **Airlink bus** to the airport from Waverley Bridge, **T** 555 6363, www.flybybus.com Fares are £3.30 single for adults, £2 for children. An open return is £5 for adults, £3 for children. Tickets can be bought from the driver or at the Tourist Information Centre (see p30). The journey time is 25 minutes, though this will be longer during the rush hour. Buses leave from Waverley Bridge every 10-20 minutes and every 10-20 minutes from the airport to the city centre from 0450 till 0025. The main pick up/drop off points in town are at the West End of Princes Street and Haymarket Station. Outside these times the N22 night bus service runs to the airport from St Andrew Square bus station. One of the white airport taxis to the city centre from the airport will cost around £16, while a black taxi cab will cost around £13-14. Journey time is roughly 20-30 minutes.

Bus

There are direct buses from most British cities to Edinburgh. The main operator is **National Express**, T 0870-5808080, www.nationalexpress.com   Tickets can be bought at bus stations or from a huge number of agents throughout the country. Fares from London to Edinburgh start at £28 for an economy advance return. From Manchester it takes 6½ hours and costs from £21 return. There are also student discounts and passes for families and those travelling over a period of days that offer substantial savings. The new bus station in St Andrew Square is the terminal for all regional and national buses.

Car

There are two main routes to Edinburgh from the south: the M1/A1 in the east; and the M6 in the west. The journey north from London takes around eight to 10 hours. A slower but more scenic route is to head off the A1 and take the A68 through the Borders.

Train

Two companies operate direct services from London King's Cross to Edinburgh Waverley: **GNER**, T 0845-7225225, www.gner.co.uk; and **Virgin**, T 0845-7222333, www.virgin.com Fares from London start at £29 return. Trains from Birmingham take 5½ hours and cost from £29 return, and from Newcastle take 1½ hours and cost from

£23 return. **Scotrail**, T 0845-7550033, www.scotrail.co.uk, operate the Caledonian Sleeper service which travels overnight from London Euston to Edinburgh and takes seven hours. There are a variety of railcards which give discounts on fares for certain groups. For information on all rail services and fares call **National Rail Enquiries**, T 0845-7484950. You can book tickets online at www.thetrainline.co.uk

Eurostar, T 0990-186186, www.eurostar.com, operates high-speed trains through the Channel Tunnel to London Waterloo from Paris (three hours) and Brussels (two hours 40 minutes). You then have to change trains, and stations, for the onward journey north to Edinburgh. If you're driving from continental Europe you could take Le Shuttle, which takes you and your car from Calais to Folkestone in 35-45 minutes.

Getting around

Bus

Public transport is generally good and efficient. It can also be expensive, but there's a whole raft of discount passes and tickets which can save you a lot of money. Two companies operate most bus services in and around the city. **Lothian Buses** use maroon and white double-decker buses, while **First Edinburgh** operate the same routes using green and yellow buses (for contact details, see p230). Standard single fares in the city centre range from £0.60-1, depending on the distance travelled. Tickets are bought from the driver. Lothian Buses have an exact fare only policy – no change is given. The frequency of bus service depends on the route, but generally speaking buses run every 10-15 minutes on most main routes Monday-Friday 0700-1900. Outside these peak times, services vary so it's best to check timetables from the offices

! The clock above Waverley Station is always a few minutes fast, ensuring that no one misses their train.

→ Galleries bus

Visiting all four of Edinburgh's main galleries couldn't be easier. A free bus service leaves from each gallery every hour seven days a week. The first bus leaves from the National Gallery, The Mound, at 1100 and every hour on the hour till 1600; then from the Portrait Gallery, 1 Queen Street, at 15 minutes past every hour (1115-1615); the Gallery of Modern Art, 75 Belford Road, at half past (1130-1630); and the Dean Gallery, 73 Belford Road, at 20 minutes to the hour from 1140 till the last bus back to town at 1700. The Sunday service operates from 1200.

listed on p230 in order to avoid a long wait. Princes Street is Edinburgh's main transport hub and you can get a bus to any part of the city from here. Transport information for the main sights outside the city are given under the relevant destinations.

Both companies offer **saver tickets**. Lothian Buses Daysaver offers a day's unlimited travel for £2.50 adult, £1.80 child (£1.80 for adults after 0930 Monday-Friday and all day Saturday and Sunday). These can be bought from the driver and are valid on all buses except tour buses, night buses or the Airlink. An Airsaver ticket is the same as a Daysaver, plus it offers one single journey to or from the airport; it costs £4.20 adult, £2.50 child. There's also a Ridacard which gives unlimited travel on all buses (except tour buses) for one week and costs £11 for adults.

Night buses run every hour from 0015 till 0315, leaving from Waverley Bridge. A flat fare of £2 (£1 with Ridacard) applies on all night bus routes and allows one transfer to another Night Bus at Waverley Bridge free of charge.

Car

Edinburgh is one of the least car-friendly cities in Britain. The main routes into town have been turned into Greenways, which give buses priority, and on-street parking is limited to 10 minutes. The centre of town is a complicated system of one-way streets designed to ease congestion, and the privatized traffic wardens are ruthless in their dedication to duty. Parking in or near the city centre is expensive and restrictive. It can cost £2 per hour to park in George Street. There are large NCP car parks behind Waverley train station (entered via East Market Street), beside the St James Centre (entered from Elder Street), on King Stables Road and on Morrison Street, near the junction with Lothian Road.

Cycling

This is just about the best way to get around the city, despite the hilly terrain. Many of the main roads have cycle lanes and there are plenty of cycle routes around the town and out into the countryside. For cycle hire, see p226.

Taxi

The council-imposed city taxi fares are not cheap, costing from around £3 for the shortest of trips up to around £6 from the centre to the outskirts. There are far more people wanting to get home late on Friday or Saturday night than there are cabs on the streets, so be prepared to wait, walk or book ahead.

Train

Many of the sights worth seeing around Edinburgh can be visited by Scotrail trains leaving from Waverley station. Details are given under the relevant destination. For Scotrail details, see p22.

! Edinburgh's traffic wardens are so relentless that one even issued a ticket to a hearse while it was parked outside the house of its recently deceased passenger.

All aboard
Princes Street, the aorta of the city's transport network, is included on most of the bus routes and home to Waverley train station.

Tours

Give in to your inner tourist and take a guided bus tour on board an open-top double-decker bus with a multi-lingual guide. These depart every 10-15 minutes from Waverley Bridge, the first one leaving around 0900 and the last one between 1730 and 2000, depending on the time of year. The complete tour lasts an hour, stopping at the main tourist sights including the Castle, Royal Mile, Palace of Holyroodhouse, New Town and Royal Yacht Britannia. Tickets are valid for the full day and you can hop on and off any of the company's buses at any of the stops. Also recommended, but not for those of a nervous disposition, are the many ghost tours. These last between one and two hours and take place daily throughout the year. Tickets can be booked in advance directly through the companies listed below, or at the tourist office, or simply turn up at the departure point on the night, see p28.

Boat tours
Maid of the Forth, **T** 331 4857, www.maidoftheforth.co.uk
Sealife cruises as well as Evening Cruises beneath the bridges
with jazz and folk accompaniment. The Evening Jazz and Ceilidh
cruises run throughout the summer on Friday, Saturday and
Sunday evenings. Adults £14, concessions £12. Wheelchair access.
The most interesting cruise of all, and the most popular, is the
cruise to the island of Inchcolm (see also p109). Sailings are from
April-September (daily July-September, weekends only April-June).
Cruises last three hours and include time ashore to explore the
abbey and island. Adults £11, concessions £9, children £4.50,
family £27. Tickets include admission to the abbey.

Bus tours
Guide Friday Tours, **T** 556 2244, **F** 557 4083, www.guidefriday.
com   Heritage Tour: adults £8.50, concessions £7, children (5-12
years) £2.50, family ticket £19.50 (2 adults and up to 4 children).
Britannia Tour: adults £6.50, concessions £5. Combined ticket:
adults £11, concessions £9, children £3, family £25. Tickets allow
discounts on many of the city's main attractions and can be
bought from the bus driver, the tourist office or at the Guide Friday
Tourism Centre, 133-135 Canongate.

Edinburgh Tour, **T** 555 6363, www.edinburghtour.com, run by
Lothian Buses (see p230). Adults £7.50, concessions £6, children
under 15 £2.50. Tickets can be bought from ticket sellers on
Waverley Bridge, the driver, or the travel shops on Hanover Street
or Waverley Bridge, and also allow discounts on entry into many
of the main sights. Tickets also allow free travel to Royal Yacht
Britannia, the Zoo and the Royal Botanic Garden.

Mac Tours, **T** 220 0770, www.mactours.com   Their Royal
Edinburgh Ticket offers a two-day hop-on hop-off service on a
vintage bus and includes entry to the Castle, Holyroodhouse and

Royal Yacht Britannia. Adults £30, concessions £24, children aged 5-12 £11. They also run a Britannia Tour: adults £7, concessions £6, children £2.50.

Cycling tours

Edinburgh City Cycle Tour, **T** 07966-447206, www.pedalculture.com   Three-hour guided bike tours of the city, leaving from the gates of Holyrood palace daily at 1000 and 1430. £15 per person.

Scottish Cycle Safaris, 29 Blackfriars St, Edinburgh, **T** 556 5560, www.cyclescotland.co.uk   Arrange bike tours in and around Edinburgh and further afield. Prices range from £30 per person per day up to £70 and over. Also hire bikes (see p226).

Ghost tours

Auld Reekie Tours, **T** 557 4700, www.auldreekietours.co.uk Tours include the underground city, haunted vaults, pagan temple and a medieval torture exhibition. Several tours daily and nightly 1230-2200, leaving from the Tron Church. Adults £6, concessions £5, children £4.

City of the Dead Haunted Graveyard Tours, **T** 225 9044, wwwblackhart.uk.com   Very scary but also entertaining. Involves being locked in a haunted graveyard at night with the notorious Mackenzie poltergeist. Leaves nightly at 2030 and 2200 from the Royal Mile, near the Mercat Cross. Adults £6, concessions £5.

Mercat Tours, **T/F** 225 6591, www.mercattours.com   Run a variety of scary tours such as 'Ghosts & Ghouls' (1900 and 2000), the 'Ghost Hunter Trail' (2130 and 2230) and 'Hidden Underground Vaults' (1100-1600). All tours leave from the Mercat Cross by St Giles Cathedral. They also run 'The Royal Mile Walk' (at 1030) and the 'Ghost & Witches Tour' in conjunction with Robin's Tours,

T/F 557 9933, which includes a visit to the 200-year-old haunted vaults hidden deep beneath the city streets (tours from outside the Tourist Information Centre at 1900 and 2100 April-October and 1900 only November to March). All tours cost £6, except the 'Ghosts and Ghouls which is £7.50.

The Witchery Tours, **T** 225 6745, www.witcherytours.com Run the 'Ghosts & Gore' tour at 1900 and 1930 (may-August) and the 'Murder & Mystery' tour (at 2100 and 2130). Both leave from outside the Witchery by the Castle restaurant and cost £7.

Walking tours
Edinburgh Voluntary Guides, **T** 664 7180. Take small groups of tourists on free guided tours from the Castle Esplanade down to the Palace of Holyroodhouse during the Festival. Call to book or just turn up at Cannonball House (by the entrance to the Esplanade) between 1000 and 1100 and 1400 and 1500.

The Scottish Literary Tour Company, **T** 226 6665/7, **F** 226 6668, www.scot-lit-tour.co.uk Those who prefer a little libation with their guided tour should try the highly acclaimed Edinburgh Literary Pub Tour, a witty exploration of the city's distinguished literary past. The two-hour tour starts at the Beehive Inn in the Grassmarket and runs daily at 1930 from June to September, Thursday-Sunday only in April, May and October and Fridays only the rest of the year. It costs £7 per person (students £5). Tickets can be booked at the tourist office or direct. The same company runs three Rebus Tours, for fans of Ian Rankin's DI Rebus novels, or anyone interested in exploring modern Edinburgh's seamy underbelly.

Tourist information

Edinburgh's main tourist office is at 3 Princes Street on top of Waverley Market (the east end), **T** 473 3800, **F** 473 3881, www.edinburgh.org (*Apr and Oct Mon-Sat 0900-1800, Sun 1100-1800; May and Sep Mon-Sat 0900-1900, Sun 1100-1900; Jun Mon-Sat 0900-1900, Sun 1000-1900; Jul and Aug Mon-Sat 0900-2000, Sun 1000-2000; Nov-Mar Mon-Sat 0900-1800, Sun 1000-1800*). It gets very busy during the peak season and at Festival time, but has the full range of services, including currency exchange, and will book accommodation, provide travel inform- ation and book tickets for various events and excursions. They also stock a wide range of guides, maps and leaflets for all of Scotland. There's also a tourist information desk at the airport, in the international arrivals area, **T** 333 2167. (*Apr-Oct Mon-Sat 0830-2130, Sun 0930-2130; Nov-Mar Mon-Fri 0900-1800, Sat 0900-1700, Sun 0930-1700*). Another useful tourist information resource is the **Backpackers Centre**, 6 Blackfriars Street, **T** 557 9393, which will provide information about hostels and tours and will book coach tickets.

Edinburgh Castle, plus several other historic sights listed in the book, is managed by **Historic Scotland** (HS), Longmore House, Salisbury Place, **T** 668 8800, www.historic-scotland.gov.uk The **National Trust for Scotland** (NTS) run hundreds of properties around the country and also let some of them to visitors. Contact them at 26-31 Charlotte Square, **T** 243 9300, www.nts.org.uk

Maps

A detailed and comprehensive map for those wishing to explore the nooks and crannies of the Old Town is the *Ordinance Survey Edinburgh Street Atlas* (£5.99). For those wishing to venture out beyond the City Bypass and explore the wilds of the Pentland Hills, *OS Landranger Sheet 66* will set you straight.

Old Town

*Edinburgh's Old Town is the dark soul of the city – the Mr Hyde to the New Town's Dr Jekyll. This medieval Manhattan of high-rise tenements is inhabited by the ghosts of the city's seamy past: Burke and Hare, Deacon Brodie and "Bloody" Mackenzie are only some of the nefarious characters to have stained the pages of Edinburgh's history. Running down its spine is the **Royal Mile**, from the **Castle**, perched high on its rock, to the **Palace of Holyroodhouse**. The 1,984 regal yards comprise four separate streets: Castlehill, Lawnmarket, the High Street and the Canongate. Along its route is a succession of tourist attractions – some less worthy of the description than others – as well as bars, restaurants, cafés and shops selling everything from kilts to Havana cigars. This is the focus of the city's tourist activity, especially during the Festival when it becomes a mêlée of street performers, enthralled onlookers and al fresco diners and drinkers. It's easy to escape the hordes, however. South of the Royal Mile is a rabbit warren of narrow alleys and closes which are fascinating by day and downright sinister by night. Here also are many of the city's museums, including the superb **Museum of Scotland**.*

▸▸ *See Sleeping p120, Eating and drinking p141, Bars and clubs p171*

◉ Sights

★ Edinburgh Castle
T 225 9846. *Daily, Apr-Sep 0930-1800, Oct-Mar 0930-1700. Last ticket sold 45 mins before closing. Adults £8.50, concessions £6.25, children £2. Parking Nov-May only, £3. Map 2, F1, p248*

The city skyline is dominated by the Castle, sitting atop an extinct volcano, protected on three sides by steep cliffs. Until the 11th century the Castle *was* Edinburgh, but with the founding of Holyrood Abbey in 1128 and development of the royal palace

It is a precipitous city, but it is still in many ways a hidden city with its catacombs and tunnels, and citizens who don't really want to be noticed, who want to be invisible.

Ian Rankin, The Sunday Telegraph, 11 August, 2002

from the early 16th century, the Castle slipped into relative obscurity. Though largely of symbolic importance, it is worth a visit, if only for the great views over the city from the battlements.

The castle is entered from the top of the Royal Mile, via the **Esplanade**, the setting for the Military Tattoo (see p200). Dotted around the Esplanade are various memorial plaques to members of the Scottish regiments who fell in overseas wars, and several military monuments. A drawbridge leads to the 19th-century **Gatehouse**, which is flanked by modern statues of Sir William Wallace and Robert the Bruce. The main path then leads steeply up, through the Portcullis Gate, to the **Argyll Battery** then the **Mill's Mount Battery**. The steep and winding road continues up to the summit of Castle Rock and **St Margaret's Chapel**, the oldest surviving building in the castle, and probably the city itself. The tiny chapel is said to have been built by Margaret herself, but the Norman style suggests it was constructed later, most likely as a memorial by her son, King David I. In front of the chapel is the **Half Moon Battery**, which offers the best panoramic views of the city.

South of the chapel is **Crown Square**, its eastern side taken up by the **Palace**, begun in the 15th century and remodelled in the 16th century for Mary, Queen of Scots. Later, in 1617, the Palace buildings were extended with the addition of the Crown Room, where the **Honours of Scotland** are now displayed – the royal crown, the sceptre and the sword of state. There is no more potent a symbol of Scottish nationhood than these magnificent crown jewels, which were last used for the coronation of Charles II in 1651. The jewel-encrusted crown contains the circlet of gold with which Robert the Bruce was crowned at Scone in 1306, and was remade for James V in 1540. Also housed in the Crown Room is the recently installed **Stone of Destiny**, the seat on which the ancient kings of Scotland were crowned.

On the south side of the square is James IV's **Great Hall**, once the seat of the Scottish Parliament and later used for state banquets. It now houses a display of arms and armour. On the west side of the square is the 18th-century **Queen Anne Barracks**, which now contains the Scottish United Services Museum. On the north side stands the neo-Gothic Scottish National Monument, a dignified testament to the many tens of thousands of Scottish soldiers killed in the First World War. From the western end of Crown Square you can descend into the **Vaults**, a series of dark and dank chambers, once used as a prison for French captives during the Napoleonic Wars. One of the rooms contains Mons Meg, the massive iron cannon forged here in the reign of James IV (1488-1513). It was said to have had a range of nearly a mile and a half and was used for salutes on royal occasions.

● *Every day (except Sundays, Christmas Day and Good Friday) since 1851, the 'One o'clock gun' has been fired from the Mill's Mount Battery as a time-check for the city's office workers.*

Castlehill
Map 2, F2/3, p248

The narrow, uppermost part of the Royal Mile nearest the castle is known as Castlehill. Just below the Castle Esplanade is a small fountain which marks the spot where more than 300 Edinburgh women were burned as witches between 1479 and 1722. Behind the fountain rise **Ramsay Gardens**, a distinctive and picturesque late 19th-century apartment block which grew around the octagonal Goose Pie House, home of 18th-century poet Allan Ramsay. The highly desirable apartments were designed by Sir Patrick Geddes, a pioneer of architectural conservation and town planning, who created them in an attempt to regenerate the Old Town. To get a closer look, follow the road left by the Outlook Tower (see below), then turn left off this road into Ramsay Gardens. The road continues downhill to meet The Mound.

Tartan Weaving Mill and Exhibition

T 226 1555. *Mon-Sat 0900-1730, Sun 1000-1730. Free entry to Mill and a small charge for the exhibition. Map 2, F1, p248*

The Tartan Weaving Mill and Exhibition is a rather kitsch affair which is probably worth a peek if it's raining. It has a real working mill where you can see tartan being woven or try your hand at making a kilt, and a small exhibition. There's also a souvenir shop and café serving cheap snacks.

Scotch Whisky Heritage Centre

354 Castlehill, **T** T220 0441, www.whisky-heritage.co.uk *Daily Jun-Sep 0930-1800, Oct-May 1000-1800. Adults £7.50, children £3.95, concessions £5.50. Map 2, F2, p248*

Next to the Witchery by the Castle restaurant (see p143) is the Scotch Whisky Heritage Centre, where you can find out everything you ever wanted to know about Scotland's national drink. It pretty much does what it says on the label. The tour consists of a couple of short films explaining the production and blending processes, and a ride in a 'barrel' through a series of historical tableaux. The best part is the bond bar, where you can sample some of the vast range of malt whiskies on offer.

Outlook Tower and Camera Obscura

T 226 3709, info@camera-obscura.demon.co.uk *Daily Apr-Oct 0930-1800 (later in Jul/Aug), Nov-Mar 1000-1700. Adults £5.75, children £3.70, concessions £4.60. Map 2, F2, p248*

A few doors further down, on the corner of Ramsay Lane, is the Outlook Tower, which has been one of the capital's top tourist attractions since a camera obscura was set up in the hexagonal tower by an optician, Maria Theresa Short, in 1854. It was then bought, in 1892, by Patrick Geddes who is best remembered for his town planning and known as 'the father of modern town planning'. He designed Edinburgh's Zoo as well as nearby Ramsay Gardens. The device consists of a giant camera which sweeps around the city and beams the live images on to a tabletop screen, accompanied by a running commentary of the city's past. There's also an exhibition of photographs taken with a variety of home-made pinhole cameras and the rooftop viewing terrace offers fantastic views of the city.

Tolbooth Kirk
Ticket centre, **T** 473 2000. *Mon-Sat 0930-1730. Map 2, F3, p248*

A little further down on the opposite side of the street is the Tolbooth Kirk, whose distinctive spire is the highest in the city. The Victorian Gothic church was designed by James Gillespie Graham, with the spire and superb interiors by Augustus Pugin, famed for his work on the House of Commons in London. It has recently been converted into The Hub, which houses the ticket centre for the Edinburgh International Festival (see p198). The Hub also stages its own exhibitions, music events and workshops, details of which are given in its own quarterly news and events brochure. Also here is Café Hub (see p149), a great eating, meeting and drinking place.

Lawnmarket
Map 2, F3-E6, p248

The Tolbooth Kirk and Assembly Hall mark the top of the Lawn-market, a much broader street than Castlehill and named after the old linen market which was held here. Today, many of the shops

! In Riddle's Court is the late 16th-century house of Bailie
● McMorran, who was shot dead by pupils of the Royal High School in 1595 during a riot against the proposed reduction in school holidays.

here still sell woven and woollen goods, as well as some embarrassing tartan tat. At the northern end is **Milne's Court**, site of the neo-Gothic New College and Assembly Hall. Built in 1859, it is the meeting place of the annual General Assembly of the Church of Scotland and also used during the Festival to stage major drama productions. It is now the temporary home for the Scottish Parliament. Next comes **James Court**, a very prestigious address, where the philosopher David Hume lived and where the poet, critic and lexicographer, Dr Johnson, was entertained in 1773 by his biographer, Boswell.

● *You can arrange tickets to visit the Debating Chamber when Parliament is sitting (Wednesday afternoons and Thursdays) at the Visitor Centre, on the corner of the Royal Mile and George IV Bridge.*

Gladstone's Land

477b Lawnmarket, **T** 226 5856. *1 Apr-31 Oct Mon-Sat 1000-1700, Sun 1400-1700, last admission 1630. Adults £3.50, concessions £2.60, children fee if accompanied by an adult. Map 2, F3, p248*

Gladstone's Land is the most important surviving example of 17th-century tenement housing in the Old Town, where the cramped conditions meant that extension was only possible in depth or upwards. The magnificent six-storey building, completed in 1620, contains remarkable painted ceilings and was the home of an Edinburgh burgess, Thomas Gledstanes. The reconstructed shop booth on the ground floor has replicas of 17th-century goods and the first floor of the house has been refurbished as a typical Edinburgh home of the period. It is managed by the National Trust for Scotland.

Writer's Museum

Lady Stair's Close, **T** 529 4901, www.cac.org.uk *Mon-Sat 1000-1700, Sun (during the Festival only) 1400-1700. Free. Map 2, F3, p248*

Lady Stair's House is another fine 17th-century house, though restored in pseudo-medieval style. It is now the home of the Writer's Museum, which celebrates the life and work of the three giants of Scottish literature: Robert Burns, Sir Walter Scott and Robert Louis Stevenson. The collection of portraits, manuscripts and various memorabilia includes Burns' writing desk, Scott's chessboard and the printing press on which his Waverley novels were produced. Other important Scottish writers, including contemporary authors, are featured in the museum's programme of temporary exhibitions. Appropriately enough, Lady Stair's Close is also where Robert Burns stayed during his first visit to the city, in 1786.

● *Further down the street on the same side is Brodie's Close, named after the father of one of Edinburgh's most nefarious characters, Deacon Brodie, see p238*

High Kirk of St Giles

High St, **T** 225 9442, dramatic@hotmail.com *Easter-Sep Mon-Fri 0900-1900, Sat 0900-1700, Sun 1300-1700, Oct-Easter Mon-Sat 0900-1700, Sun 1300-1700. Free (donations welcome).* Map 2, F4, p248

The High Kirk of St Giles has had a colourful past ever since medieval times when the Scottish Parliament met here. It was the launch pad for the Reformation, then, around the turn of the 16th century, it was divided up and used as law courts, the town clerk's office, a school and a prison. When the High Kirk returned to its religious function it was partitioned into four different churches, each serving its own congregation, finally being reunified after its Victorian restoration. One of the most celebrated incidents in the church's history happened in 1637, when an attempt to read from

---

! In the 18th century Old Town people were still in the habit
● of throwing their refuse and sewage out of the tenement windows, shouting to passers-by below the traditional warning "Gardyloo" (from the French *garde à l'eau*).

Sex and drugs and body and soul
Cockburn Street presents a grungier side to the city.

the English prayer book so incensed Jenny Geddes, a humble stall-holder, that she launched her stool at the bishop's head. A plaque marks the spot where it hit and records the ensuing riot. Such disturbances led to the National Covenant of 1638, establishing the Presbyterian Church of Scotland in defiance of Charles I. This in turn led to Civil War, during which many Covenanters were imprisoned in the church. There have been many additions to the High Kirk since its restoration. One of these is the very beautiful **Thistle Chapel**, the Chapel of the Most Ancient and Most Noble Order of the Thistle (Scotland's foremost order of chivalry). It was designed by Sir Robert Lorimer and built in 1911. The elaborate ornamentation and fine carvings are exquisite (look out for the angel playing the bagpipes). Guides can explain the chapel's history and significance. There are also several Pre-Raphaelite stained-glass windows in the church, and above the west door is a memorial window to Robert Burns, rather surprising given that he was hardly an upholder of Presbyterian values. There's also a café-restaurant, The Lower Aisle, in the crypt (see p150), which can be reached from stairs outside the Thistle Chapel.

Parliament Square
Map 2, F4/5, p248

The High Kirk of St Giles forms the northern side of Parliament Square which is also surrounded by the Law Courts, Parliament House and the Signet Library. The **Law Courts**, where Sir Walter Scott practised as an advocate, were originally planned by architect Robert Adam (1728-92), who contributed so much to the grace and elegance of the New Town, but, due to lack of funds, built to designs by Robert Reid (1776-1856). On the west side of the square

! Should you see passers-by spitting on the Heart of Midlothian, it is not a sign of disrespect, but supposed to bring good luck

is the **Signet Library**, centre for the Society of Her Majesty's Writers to the Signet, an organization that originated from the 15th-century Keepers of the King's Seal, or signet. It boasts one of the finest neoclassical interiors in the city, but unfortunately can only be seen by prior written application, except on very occasional open days. **Parliament House**, facing the south side of St Giles, was the meeting place of the Scots Parliament between 1639 and 1707. It is now used by the city's lawyers in between court sittings, but is readily accessible during the week. The most notable feature is the magnificent **Parliament Hall** with its 17th-century hammerbeam roof. In front of the west door of the church is the site of the city Tolbooth, demolished in 1817, and now marked by a heart-shaped pattern in the cobblestones, known as the Heart of Midlothian and made famous by Sir Walter Scott in his eponymous novel. Behind the church is the **Mercat Cross**, where public proclamations are traditionally read. The present cross is a replica, gifted by then prime minister, WE Gladstone.

The Real Mary King's Close
High St, entrance on Warriston's Close, www.realmarykingsclose. com *Tours daily every 20 mins from 1000. Apr-Oct last tour at 2100; Nov-Mar last tour at 1600. Adults £7, concessions £6, children 5-15 £5. No children under 5. There are steep and uneven sections; disabled visitors should call in advance; **T** 08702-430160. Map 2, E5, p248*

Opposite St Giles is **Edinburgh City Chambers**, designed by John Adam (brother of Robert) and built in 1753 as the Royal Exchange. In the early 19th century it became the headquarters of the city council. Beneath the city chambers is Mary King's Close, closed off for many years after the 1645 plague which killed most of the inhabitants. When the plague struck, the Close was abandoned and the houses sealed to prevent the spread of the disease. The building of the Royal Exchange was welcomed as an opportunity to end the fear and superstition associated with the Close's legacy. The infamous street remains virtually intact and has recently been re-opened as a tourist attraction, offering an authentic insight into trials and tribulations of 17th century Old Town life.

Cockburn Street
Map 2, E5/6, p248 See also p201

The steep, cobbled slope of Cockburn Street presents a grungier side of Edinburgh, with fetish clothing shops, piercing parlours and second-hand record shops. There are also some good bars and restaurants as well as the **Stills Gallery** (**T** 622 6200. *Tue-Sat 1000-1700*) and the **Collective Gallery** (**T** 220 1260).

Edinburgh Dungeon
Market St, **T** 0870-8460666, www.thedungeons.com *Nov-Mar Mon-Fri 1100-1600, Sat/Sun 1030-1630; Apr-Jun daily 1000-1700; Jul-Aug 1000-1900; Sep-Oct 1000-1700. Adults £7.95, concessions £5.95. Map 2, E4, p248*

Next to Waverley Station is the new Edinburgh Dungeon, an entertaining trawl through some of the more sinister and infamous characters in Scottish history and there's an Edinburgh section on the likes of Burke and Hare and Deacon Brodie. It's all very scary and not for the squeamish, but tends to paint its historical detail with a very broad brush.

City Arts Centre and Fruitmarket Gallery
City Arts Centre: 2 Market St, **T** 529 3993, www.cac.org.uk *Mon-Sat 1000-1700, also Sun 1400-1700 in Jul/Aug. Free (charges for special exhibitions).* Fruitmarket Gallery, **T** 225 2383. *Mon-Sat 1100-1800, Sun 1200-1700. Free. Map 2, E5 and D5, p248*

The City Arts Centre is an excellent municipal art space with a large collection of Scottish works, including those by McTaggart,

Fergusson, Peploe and Eardley. There's also an ever-changing programme of exhibitions which is often innovative, inspired and community based, covering an eclectic mix of themes, from rare Egyptian antiquities to Star Trek. On the ground floor is the City Art Centre Café (see p149). Opposite the City Art Centre is the smaller and more contemporary Fruitmarket Gallery. Their friendly café is a good place to linger (see p150).

Tron Kirk
Map 2, E6, p248

At the junction of the High Street and South Bridge is the Tron Kirk, founded in 1637, and now more famously known as a favourite Hogmanay rendezvous. The church was built to accommodate the Presbyterian congregation ejected from St Giles during the latter's brief period as a cathedral and was originally T-shaped, but had to be cut down in size in the late 18th century in order to make way for North and South Bridge. It was later changed once more when the old steeple and roof were damaged in the 'great conflagration', a terrible fire in the Old Town in 1824. The church continued in use as a place of worship until it was closed in 1952 owing to a declining congregation. It now houses the Old Town Tourist Information Centre, which has lots of information as well being the site of the excavation of an original Old Town Close.

● *Past the junction of the North and South Bridges, on the north side of the High Street, is Carruber's Close, where Sir James Simpson, the discoverer of chloroform, ran a medical dispensary in the 1860s.*

Brass Rubbing Centre
Chalmers Close, **T** 556 4364. *Apr-Sep, Mon-Sat 1000-1700; Sun 1200-1700 (during the Festival only). Free. Map 2, E7, p249*

Housed in the Trinity Apse is the Brass Rubbing Centre, where you can make your own rubbings from the materials supplied. No experience is required and the staff are ready to help. The Trinity Apse is the only surviving fragment of the Trinity College Church, one of Edinburgh's finest pieces of Gothic architecture, founded circa 1460 by Queen Mary of Gueldres, wife of James II of Scotland. It was demolished in 1848 to make room for the railway line.

Museum of Childhood

42 High St, **T** 529 4142. *Mon-Sat 1000-1700, Sun in Jul-Aug 1200-1700. Free. Map 2, E7, p249*

The Museum of Childhood is full of kids screaming with excitement at the vast collection of toys, dolls, games and books, and nostalgic adults yelling "I used to have one of those!" There's even a video history of the various Gerry Anderson TV puppet series such as Thunderbirds and Fireball XL5. The museum also covers the serious issues of childhood, such as health and education, but that doesn't spoil the fun. The only downside is the part where you start to recognize toys from your own childhood and realize just how dated they look. Will today's kids come here in 30 years and feel nostalgic for GameBoys? Now there's a scary thought!

John Knox House

43-45 High St, **T** 556 9579. *Mon-Sat 1000-1600, last admission 1630. Also Sun 1200-1700 in Jul-Aug. Adults £2.25, concessions £1.75, children under 15 £0.75. Map 2, E7, p249*

Dating from the late 15th century and added to in the 16th century, John Knox's House is one of the Royal Mile's most distinctive buildings. It's not known for sure whether or not the firebrand Calvinist preacher actually lived here, but the house did belong to

! The Tron Kirk is named after the Tron, a public weighing beam which stood close by. Merchants found guilty of selling short measures were nailed to the Tron by their ears.

Subterranean spirits

Be afraid – be very afraid...The spirits who haunt the vaults and tunnels of old Edinburgh have drawn tourists to the capital over the years. But recent research has revealed that there may be something really going on beneath the city's streets. A comprehensive study into paranormal activity was carried out as part of the Edinburgh International Science Festival. Over 250 volunteers, who were unaware of the history of the vaults, entered the network of ancient tunnels and reported greatly increased paranormal activity, such as seeing figures, hearing loud breathing and being touched or grabbed.

James Mossman, goldsmith to Mary, Queen of Scots. Today, it is a museum to the man's life and career, but though the house itself is interesting, the displays are one-dimensional and rather austere.

Canongate
Map 2, E8-D12, p249

The High Street ends at the junction of St Mary's Street and Jeffrey Street, where the city's eastern gate, **Netherbow Port**, once stood. The remaining part of the Royal Mile, the Canongate, was a separate burgh for over 700 years, taking its name from the canons (priests) of Holyrood Abbey. As it was near the Palace of Holyroodhouse, the area developed as the court quarter with several fine residences being built there. Though the Canongate went into decline once the court moved to London in the early 17th century, it could still boast an impressive number of aristocrats among its inhabitants, even in the late 18th century. Many of the buildings in the Canongate have been ambitiously restored in recent decades. One of the most lavish of the Canongate's mansions was the 17th-century **Moray House**, visited on several occasions by Charles I and used by Cromwell as his headquarters in 1648. And if that weren't enough historical significance, in 1707 the Act of Union was signed in a summerhouse in the garden.

Museum of Edinburgh

142 Canongate, **T** 529 4143. *Mon-Sat 1000-1700 and Sun 1400-1700 during the Festival. Free. Map 2, D10, p249*

The city's official local history museum is housed in 16th-century Huntly House. Though the collection is disparate and initially disappointing, it gets better upstairs. Among the highlights is the original copy of the National Covenant of 1638, which appealed for an end to royal control over parliament, and Greyfriars Bobby's collar.

The People's Story Museum

163 Canongate, **T** 529 4057. *Mon-Sat 1000-1700, Sun 1400-1700 during the Festival. Free. Map 2, D10, p249*

Opposite Huntly House is the late 16th-century Canongate Tolbooth, the original headquarters of the burgh administration, as well as the courthouse and burgh prison. It now houses this museum which offers a fascinating insight into the lives of ordinary Edinburgh folk from the late 18th century to the present day. It is evocative, disturbing and entertaining in equal measure, and if you don't feel a deep sense of compassion at the truly appalling condditions many people lived in, then you've got a heart of stone. The museum is filled with the sights, sounds and smells of the past and includes reconstructions of a prison cell, a workshop and a pub, among others.

Canongate Kirk

Map 2, D10, p249

Next door to the Tolbooth is the Canongate Kirk, built in 1688 to house the congregation expelled from Holyrood Abbey when it

Cannibal spectre

On the night of the signing of the Act of Union in 1707, one of the young servants was working in the kitchen of Queensberry House, preparing the celebration feast that was to follow the signing of the treaty. James' eldest son, Lord Drumlanrig, who was so insane he had to be kept locked up, escaped from his room and ran the young kitchen lad through with a sword. He then spit-roasted him in one of the kitchen fireplaces and was sitting munching away when he was found later by the returning party.

was taken over by James VII (II of England) to be used as the chapel for the Order of the Thistle. More interesting is the churchyard, burial place of many famous people. Among the list of notable names is Adam Smith, the father of political economy, who lived in Panmure House nearby, the philosopher Dugald Stewart, and the poet Robert Fergusson, who died tragically at the tender age of 23 after being forced into the local madhouse during a bout of depression. Robert Burns, who was greatly inspired by Fergusson's poetry, donated the headstone in 1787, inscribed with his own personal tribute.

● *Beside the Canongate Kirk, Dunbar's Close leads to Dunbar Close Garden, an attractive, secluded spot with good views up to the Royal High School and Calton Hill.*

Canongate Kirk to Holyrood
Map 2, D10-12, p249

Further down the hill is the north side of the magnificent new Scottish Parliament building (see p52) which cleverly incorporates **Queensberry House**, built in 1681 for Lord Hatton, but later bought by William first Duke of Queensberry. William's son, James, was the Secretary of State and architect of the Act of Union of 1707 between Scotland and England. He accepted a bribe of £12,000 to push through the treaty, thus ending Scotland's independence. Needless to say, it did not go down too well with many Scots. At the foot of the Canongate, is **White Horse Close**, restored in 1964 and named after Mary, Queen of Scots' white palfrey. The stables for Holyroodhouse are thought to have been located here, and later the coaching inn from where stagecoaches began the journey south to London. The last few yards of the Royal Mile forms the approach to the precincts of Holyrood Abbey and Palace and is known as the **Abbey Strand**. The strange little turreted 16th-century building here is known as Queen Mary's Bath House, where Mary is reputed to have bathed in sweet white wine.

Palace of Holyroodhouse

T 556 1096, www.royal.gov.uk *Daily 1 Apr-31 Oct 0930-1800 (last admission 1715); 1 Nov-31 Mar 0930-1630 (last admission 1545; by guided tour only). Closed to the public during state functions and during the annual royal visit in the last two weeks of Jun and first week in Jul. Adults £6.50, concessions £5, children £3.30, family £16.50. Map 2, C13, p249*

At the foot of the Royal Mile lies Holyrood, Edinburgh's royal quarter. Holyroodhouse began life as the abbey guesthouse, until James IV transformed it into a royal palace at the beginning of the 16th century. The only remaining part of the Renaissance palace is the northwest tower, built as the private apartments of his son James V. Most of the original building was damaged by fire in 1543, and further damaged in 1650 during its occupation by Cromwell's troops, never the most considerate of guests. The present palace largely dates from the late 17th century when the original was replaced by a larger building for the Restoration of Charles II, although the newly crowned monarch never actually set foot in the place. It was built in the style of a French château, around a large arcaded quadrangle, and is an elegant, finely proportioned creation, designed by William Bruce. Inside, the oldest part of Holyroodhouse is open to the public and is entered through the **Great Gallery**, which takes up the entire first floor of the north wing. The most interesting part of the palace is the **Royal Apartments** in the northwest tower, in particular the bedchamber of Mary, Queen of Scots, scene of the most infamous incident in the palace's long history. It was here that the queen witnessed the brutal murder, organized by her jealous husband, Lord Darnley, of her much-favoured Italian private secretary, David Rizzio. He was stabbed 56 times, on a spot marked by a brass plaque and, until it was removed quite recently, by a distinctly unsubtle fake bloodstain. Also here is a collection of bits and pieces from various monarchs, including a cast of Robert the Bruce's skull and a lock of Mary, Queen of Scots' hair.

The later parts of the palace, known as the **State Apartments**, are less interesting, though decorated in Adam Style, with magnificent white stucco ceilings, particularly the **Throne Room** and **Dining Room**. These are associated with later monarchs, such as George IV, who paid a visit in 1822, dressed in flesh-coloured tights and the briefest of kilts, rather appropriately perhaps, given the length of time he actually spent here. But it was Queen Victoria and Prince Albert who returned the palace to royal favour, as a stopover on their way to and from Balmoral. The Palace is still the monarch's official residence in Edinburgh and the present Queen still spends a short while here every year at the end of June and beginning of July.

In the grounds of the palace are the crumbling ruins of **Holyrood Abbey**, most of which date from the early 13th century. The abbey was, at its height, a building of great importance and splendour, and this is hinted at in the surviving parts of the west front. Much of it was destroyed, as were many of the country's finest ecclesiastical buildings, during the Reformation. During the reign of Charles I it was converted to the Chapel Royal and later to the Chapel of the Order of the Thistle, but it suffered severe damage once more, this time during the 1688 revolution. Some restoration work was attempted in the 18th century, but this only caused the roof to collapse in 1768, and since then the building has been left to rot. In the Royal Vault beneath the abbey are buried several Scottish Kings, including David II (son of Robert the Bruce), James II and James V.

Scottish Parliament
Visitor Centre daily 1000-1600. Free. Map 2, D11/12, p249

Opposite the Palace of Holyroodhouse is the new Scottish Parliament building, still under construction at the time of going to press but scheduled for completion by the end of 2003. The controversial building was designed by visionary Barcelona architect, Enric Miralles, who died in 2000, the same year that Donald Dewar, architect of the Scottish Parliament and the first First Minister of Scotland, also died. It incorporates symbols of Scottish economic and artistic heritage: the roof is a series of up-turned fishing boats, while the windows are based on an abstract shape of Sir Henry Raeburn's *Skater on Duddingston Loch*, and the crow-stepped gables are a paradigm of Scots vernacular architecture married to modernist principles. The fact that the new building also incorporates Queensberry House (see p49) only adds to the potent symbolism. The parliament building has not been without its critics, however, in particular over the spiraling costs, which now stand at nearly £400 mn. The adjoining visitor centre includes the original architectural designs and models and a 15-minute film of its development from the conceptual stage. Until the building is complete (late 2003), the Scottish Parliament sits in the Church of Scotland headquarters in Milne's Court (see p39). A visitor centre on George IV Bridge provides information about the workings of the parliament (**T** 348 5411, www.scottish.parliament.uk).

★ **Dynamic Earth**

Holyrood Rd, **T** 550 7800, www.dynamicearth.co.uk *Apr-Oct daily 1000-1800; Nov-Mar Wed-Sun 1000-1700 (last admission 1550). Adults £8.45, children and concessions £4.95, family (2 adults, 2 kids) £22.50. Map 2, D12, p249 See also Kids p223.*

Edinburgh's very own mini-dome. This multi-million pound, multi-media exhibition takes you on a journey through space and time. The journey begins with the State of the Earth, which shows erupting volcanoes, earthquakes and extreme weather conditions around the globe on giant video screens. Next up is the Time Machine section which takes you back through history, all the way to the dinosaurs and beyond to when it all started. Then you get to play Captain Kirk, standing on the bridge of a starship watching the Big Bang in spectacular fashion. Fasten your seatbelts next for a simulated flight over glaciers and icebergs and U-shaped valleys as you experience Shaping the Surface. Then it's on to the Earth's casualty ward and a roll call of all those animals who have fallen prey to man, before passing through displays of the Earth's different climatic zones. The climax to the journey comes with an audiovisual presentation which is part disaster movie-part environmental lecture. On the top deck is a well-run, family-oriented self-service café, a bar serving drinks and sandwiches, several takeaway kiosks, and outside seating in summer.

Cowgate

Map 2, G4-F10, p250-251

The Cowgate is one of Edinburgh's oldest streets and one of its least salubrious. It runs almost parallel to the High Street, but on a much lower level, and when the South and George IV bridges were built over it, linking the Old and New Towns, it was half-buried below street level and reduced to a dark, desolate canyon of neglect and decay. In recent years the Cowgate has become one of the city's major nightlife streets, lined with bars and clubs and packed full of drunken revellers at weekends. In December 2002 the street hit the headlines when it went up in flames. Though the fire gutted the much-loved Gilded Balloon Comedy Club, a favourite Festival venue, it was extinguished before it spread to the rest of the Old Town, thus narrowly averting a potential disaster.

St Cecilia's Hall

Cowgate and Niddry St. *Wed and Sat 1400-1700. £3. Map 2, F7, p249 See also Arts and entertainment, p191*

There are a couple of very notable and very interesting buildings on Cowgate such as the exquisite St Cecilia's Hall, built in 1763 for the Edinburgh Musical Society. The interior, modelled on the opera house at Parma, is stunning, with an oval music hall and concave elliptical ceiling. In the 18th century it was the city's main concert hall, and since its restoration in 1966 has again been used as a venue for concerts, especially during the Festival. The Hall also houses the Russell Collection of early keyboard instruments for Edinburgh University's Music Department.

Magdalen Chapel

Cowgate, **T** 220 1450. *Mon-Fri 0930-1600; other times by arrangement only. Free. Map 2, G4, p248*

Further west along the Cowgate is Magdalen Chapel, founded in 1541. The unremarkable façade is Victorian but the fine interior is Jacobean and worth a look, in particular to see the only extant pre-Reformation Scottish stained-glass window in the country.

Burke and Hare

Two of Edinburgh's most notorious murderers were William Burke and William Hare, who first met in 1826 in a boarding house in Tanner's Close in the West Port. Their chilling career began after the death of one of the tenants. At that time local surgeons were willing to pay good money for fresh corpses and the pair sold a deceased fellow tenant's body to Doctor Knox, an eminent Professor of Anatomy. Soon after, another opportunity presented itself when another lodger was taken ill. This time, the murderous pair helped speed up the process by suffocating him. Again they sold the body to Doctor Knox. Now they would have to go out hunting for victims if they were to continue. So they lured an old woman, a salt seller from Gilmerton, back to Tanner's Close, where they plied her with drink till unconscious. Then they strangled her, before once more carting the body up to Doctor Knox's dissecting rooms. More murders followed, but it was only a matter of time before their growing bloodlust and complacency would lead to their downfall. It finally happened when two beggars who were staying at the same boarding house discovered a woman's blood-spattered body hidden under a pile of hay in their room. They alerted the police who duly arrived to find the pair drinking and singing, the dead body still in the room. The trial of William Burke took place on 24 December 1828. Among the witnesses for the prosecution was William Hare who had turned king's evidence. Burke was sentenced to death and hanged before a crowd of 20,000 on 28 January 1829. His partner in crime, William Hare, was forced to leave the city, and died later in a miserable cellar in the East End of London. Doctor Knox meanwhile left Edinburgh and became an alcoholic and down and out in London.

Grassmarket
Map 2, H2-G4, p248

The Cowgate passes beneath George IV Bridge to become the
Grassmarket, a wide cobbled street closed in by tall tenements
and dominated by the Castle looming overhead. The Grassmarket,
formerly the city's cattle market, has been the scene of some of
the more notorious incidents in the city's often dark and grisly
past. The public gallows were located here and over 100 hanged
Covenanters are commemorated with a cross at its east end. It
was in the Grassmarket, in 1763, where the Porteous Riots took
place, when an angry mob lynched Captain Porteous, the officer in
charge of the city guard. Today, the Grassmarket is one of the city's
main nightlife centres. There are several good restaurants but it's
primarily a boozing street, with a line of popular drinking holes
along its north side, making it the perfect place for a pub crawl.
This fact is not lost on the hordes of visiting hen and stag parties
that descend on the city every weekend for a couple of nights on
the razzle, turning the Grassmarket once more into a giant cattle
market. Several hotels cater for this growing trade by offering
good value weekend bed-and-breakfast deals (see Sleeping, p120).

At its western end, the Grassmarket forks: the left prong, the
West Port, leads up towards Tollcross, while the right prong, King
Stables Road, leads to the bottom end of Lothian Road. The area
around the West Port is better known locally as the 'Pubic Triangle',
owing to the preponderence of sleazy lap dancing bars and strip
joints. Around here, in the now vanished Tanner's Close, is where
Burke and Hare lured their hapless murder victims, whose bodies
they then sold to the city's medical schools (see p55). Dancing
of a more highbrow nature takes place in **Dance Base**, the new
national centre for dance in Scotland, see p190.

Victoria Street
Map 2, G3, p248

At the northeastern corner of the Grassmarket is Victoria Street, an attractive two-tiered street with a pedestrian terrace above. Victoria Street is best known for its range of more unusual shops, specializing in everything from brushes to cheese. There are also some good restaurants here. Victoria Street curves up from the Grassmarket to George IV Bridge and the **National Library of Scotland**, founded in 1682 and one of the largest public libraries in the UK. It holds a rich collection of early printed books and manuscripts, historical documents and the letters and papers of notable national literary figures, which are displayed for the public (*Mon-Sat 1000-1700, free*).

Greyfriars Kirk and Kirkyard
Map 2, H4, p248

Greyfriars Kirkyard is one of Edinburgh's most prestigious burial grounds. Here lie the poet Allan Ramsay, the architects John and Robert Adam, the philanthropist George Heriot (see p59), James Douglas, Earl of Morton and Regent of Scotland during James VI's minority, and the poet Duncan Ban McIntyre (1724-1812). The graveyard also gave its name to Edinburgh's most famous four-legged son (see p59). Aside from its glamorous historical connections, Greyfriars also has its infamous stories. Wandering around the graveyard, you'll notice that some of the memorials are protected with metal lattices. This was to defeat the efforts of body snatchers. One woman was buried here while in a trance and awoke when body snatchers tried to remove the rings from her

! Greyfriars inspired Charles Dickens' classic 'A Christmas Carol'. Dickens had been reading the inscriptions on tombstones and misread 'Mr Scroggie, a meal man' as 'Mr Scrooge, a mean man'. A meal man was a grain merchant in those days.

Dogged determination
Greyfriars Bobby, the city's great canine icon, took the notion of a graveside vigil to new and improbable lengths.

fingers. But most notorious of all is the tale of George "Bloody" Mackenzie, former Lord Advocate, who is interred here. Greyfriars is particularly associated with the long struggle to establish the Presbyterian church in Scotland. The kirkyard was the first place where the National Covenant was signed, on 28 February 1638. Later, in 1679, over 1,200 Covenanters were imprisoned by Mackenzie in a corner of the kirkyard for three months, and many died of exposure and starvation. The prison, known as the **Black Mausoleum**, is behind the church, on the left, and is said to be haunted by the evil presence of Mackenzie's spirit. Those brave enough to visit the Black Mausoleum under cover of darkness as part of one of the ghost tours (see p28) are guaranteed an evening to remember. **Greyfriars Kirk**, somewhat overshadowed by the graveyard, dates from 1620 and was the first church to be built

A dog's life

At the top of Candlemaker Row by the entrance to Greyfriars is the statue of Greyfriars Bobby, the faithful little Skye terrier who watched over the grave of his master John Gray, a shepherd from the Pentland Hills, for 14 years until his own death in 1872. The grave that Bobby watched over is in Greyfriars Kirkyard. During this time Bobby became something of a local celebrity and was cared for by locals, who even gave him his own collar, and every day, on hearing the One o'clock gun, he would go to the local pub (now named in his honour) to be fed. By the time of his death, his fame had spread to such an extent that Queen Victoria herself suggested that he be buried beside his master. The little statue, modelled from life and erected soon after his death, is one of the most popular, and sentimental, of Edinburgh's attractions, thanks to a number of movies of the wee dog's life.

Edinburgh

in Edinburgh after the Reformation. It's an odd mix of styles, with Gothic windows and buttresses taken from the nearby Franciscan Friary and a second church joined on to the west end in 1722. In 1938 the dividing wall between the two churches was removed, creating one long spireless church.

George Heriot's School
Map 2, H2/3, p248

West of Greyfriars Kirkyard, and reached from Lauriston Place, is George Heriot's Hospital School, one of the finest pieces of renaissance architecture in Scotland. It was founded as a school for the teaching of "puir fatherless bairns" in 1659 by "Jinglin' Geordie" Heriot, James VI's goldsmith, although it had previously been used as a hospital by Cromwell during the Civil War. It is now one of

Edinburgh's most prestigious fee-paying schools. You can't go inside but you can wander round the quadrangle and admire the towers, turrets and carved doorways of this fine palatial building.

★ Museum of Scotland

Chambers St, **T** 247 4422, www.nms.ac.uk *Mon-Sat 1000-1700, Tue till 2000, Sun 1200-1700. Free. Guided tours daily at 1415 and at 1800 on Tue. Themed tours daily at 1515, leaving from the main concourse, and lasting 45 mins. Soundguides are available from the ticket desk. Commentaries also in French and German, £2. Map 2, H4, p248*

The Museum of Scotland is a treasure trove of intriguing and important artefacts, including Roman gold and silver, Pictish and Gaelic carved stones, medieval armour and "The Maiden", Edinburgh's once-busy guillotine. The displays run chronologically from the basement up to the sixth floor, beginning with, appropriately enough, Beginnings and Early People. Straight off, from Paolozzi's sculptures holding ancient relics, you know this is going to be a far cry from the musty, austere museum visits of childhood. Levels 1 (street level) and 2 are entitled the Kingdom of the Scots which takes us through Scotland's emergence as a nation, then Level 3 – Scotland Transformed – runs from the Union of the Scots and English Parliaments in 1707 to the industrial age. Upwards and onwards to Industry and Empire on Levels 4 and 5 which explores Scotland's role in shipbuilding, technical innovation and empire building. Finally, on the top floor, the 20th century is dealt with in a completely innovative way with a selection of objects by famous and ordinary Scots, though it won't have escaped everyone's notice that the more interesting items were chosen by the less-than-famous. They range from the sadistic (a leather tawse) to the humorous (glow-in-the-dark condoms) via the conceited (Kirsty Wark's Saab). Though the collection is at times a patchy, incomplete picture of Scottish history, there is a vast amount to see and it presents its displays in a clear and logical manner, giving an accessible overview of the story of this nation. Moreover, the building itself is a joy to explore and offers some great surprises, such as the frequent walk-throughs to the Royal Museum. Don't miss a trip to the roof terrace, from where the views across the city are special.

● *The Discovery Centre on Level 3 is a hands-on area aimed at kids, where they can grind corn, make pots, dress up as a Viking, or play the lute.*

★ Royal Museum of Scotland

T 247 4219. *Same opening hours as the Museum of Scotland. Free. Guided tours daily (except Thu) at 1430 and Sun at 1530. Also "quickies" for kids on Sat at 1415 and Sun at 1515. Themed tours on Thu and Sun at 1430.* Map 2, G5, p248

Royal Museum, entered from Chambers Street, holds an extensive and eclectic range of collections on display and includes everything from Classical Greek sculptures to stuffed elephants and Native North American totem poles. It's all housed in a wonderful Victorian building, designed by Captain Francis Fowkes of the Royal Engineers (architect of the Royal Albert Hall in London) and built in 1888 in the style of an Italianate palace. The magnificent atrium soars high above and makes a very impressive entrance to what is probably the most complete museum in the country, divided into three general categories. **The Natural World** is arranged on all three floors and, aside from being an object lesson in the skills of taxidermy, also includes the environmentally friendly 'World in our Hands' exhibition, which explains to what extent we have destroyed our planet and how we can repair the damage. Also arranged over three floors is the **Decorative Arts**, which features an impressive collection of Oriental treasures. **Science and Industry** is also well covered, on the ground and second floors. There are cafés in the atrium and at the rear of the ground floor, also entered from Lothian Street via the Lumière Cinema (see p188).

Old College and Talbot Rice Gallery

Talbot Rice Gallery, **T** 650 2210. *Tue-Sat 1000-1700 (daily during the Fesitval). Free. There are also free lunchtime guided tours of the Old College, from 19 Jul-28 Aug, Mon-Sat, starting at 1300 at the reception. For more details of University tours, contact the University of Edinburgh Centre, 7-11 Nicolson St, **T** 650 2252. Mon-Fri 0915-1700. Map 2, G6, p248*

Hemmed in by Chambers Street, South Bridge, West College Street and South College Street is Edinburgh University Old College, whose main courtyard is reached through the massive arch on South Bridge. Built between 1789 and 1834, the Old College, was originally designed by Robert Adam, but on his death in 1792 very little had been completed and his grandiose plans had to be abandoned due to lack of funds. William Playfair was later commissioned to finish the job, in 1815. The final building is a single large court, instead of Adam's two, and its finest section is the upper library, a magnificent architectural achievement and one of the finest neoclassical interiors in Scotland. It is now mainly used for ceremonial occasions but can be viewed by guided tour in the summer. The Upper Museum, which housed the Royal Museum before it moved to its present site, is now the home of the **Talbot Rice Gallery**, which features the University's collection of Renaissance European painting as well as several temporary exhibitions every year. Some parts of the college are open to visitors, namely the Upper Library and Upper Museum.

Museum of Pathology and Anatomy

18 Nicolson St, **T** 527 1649. *Open to the public only by booking well in advance and only to groups of between 12 and 24 and to those aged 15 or over. Guides selected according to prior knowledge of the group. Map 2, H7, p249*

Victorian values

Victoria Street is where to come if you want brushes, speciality cheeses, practical jokes or pretty much anything out of the ordinary.

Almost opposite the new Edinburgh Festival Theatre is the Royal College of Surgeons, Playfair's impressive Greek Revivalist temple to all things surgical, built in 1832, and now a working museum for the study of human disease. This gruesome freak show has displays of various diseased, abnormal or deformed parts of the human body in jars and includes examples of Siamese Twins and a Chinese bound foot.

● *Next to the Royal College of Surgeons is the Old Surgeon's Hall, which it replaced, and where Burke and Hare brought their victims' bodies to sell to Dr Knox, see p55.*

★ **Sir Jules Thorn Exhibition of the History of Surgery and Dental Museum**
9 Hill Sq, **T** 527 1600, www.rcsed.ac.uk *Mon-Fri 1400-1600. Free. Buses 5, 7, 8, 21, 31/33, 80 from Princes St. Map 2, H7, p249*

Hidden behind the Royal College of Surgeon's Hall is this wee gem, which outlines the history of surgery in the city since the early 16th century. Edinburgh's contribution to medicine and surgery has been considerable to say the least, and the artefacts on display highlight the role played by such great figures as Joseph Lister (1827-1912), who discovered the benefits of antiseptic surgery, Sir Charles Bell (1774-1842), the professor of surgery who discovered the distinct functions of the nerves, and James Young Simpson (1811-70), who pioneered the use of chloroform as an anaesthetic, and to whom we must all be eternally grateful, especially after you see the frightening collection of early surgical instruments on view. Also on display is Burke's death mask and the pocket book made from the skin of his hand. Upstairs the displays focus on modern surgery, and the pictures feature much blood and gore. There's also a laparoscopy machine, which is used to teach keyhole surgery and allows visitors to try their hand at performing operations inside a mock tummy using a television screen to control various surgical instruments. The museum is well laid out,

Snatch me if you can

In the 18th century Edinburgh's surgeons were under suspicion of secretly encouraging the dubious practice of body snatching, and rightly so. In one incident, a fight broke out between the friends of a woman, Maggie Dickson, who had just been executed and some surgeons' apprentices eager to procure her fresh corpse for dissection. In the middle of the fracas the 'corpse' came to life, thereafter becoming known as 'half hangit' Maggie'. There's even a pub in Cockburn Street named after her.

informative and enormous fun, but not for the squeamish. By the entrance is the **Dental Museum**, which may appeal to students and sadists but basically consists of a load of old dental tools.

George Square and Bristo Square
Buses 23, 27, 40, 41, 42, 46 from Princes St. Map 5, D3, p254

The main campus of Edinburgh University, around George Square, does not boast the architectural kudos of the Old College. George Square is surrounded by rather ugly and functional 1960s build-ings, most notably the library, a glass and concrete eyesore which was designed by Sir Basil Spence. A few of the original buildings survive, providing scant evidence that George Square was once one of the most fashionable addresses in the city in the late 18th century, prior to the development of the New Town (Sir Walter Scott lived at No 25). Just to the north and east of George Square is Bristo Square, a favourite spot for skateboarders, surrounded by a car park, the grey box-like student centre, the Teviot Row Student Union and the University's chief ceremonial centre, **McEwan Hall**, a huge Italian-style basilica, completed in 1897, which makes up for in size what it lacks in aesthetic qualities. It was gifted to the

★ **Things for free**

Best

- Visit the Gallery of Modern Art, p88
- Have a picnic in the Botanic Garden, p85
- Visit the Museum of Scotland, p60
- Admire the views from the top of Calton Hill, p78
- Walk along the Water of Leith, p90

university by the eponymous brewing family. Behind the McEwan Hall is the **Reid Concert Hall**, built in 1858 in Italian Renaissance style and housing the **Edinburgh University Collection of Historic Musical Instruments** (*Wed 1500-1700 and Sat 1000-1300*). There are over 1,500 musical instruments from around the world, showing how each has evolved over the years, as well as the new Sound Laboratory which uses real instruments and computer read-outs to demonstrate how sound is produced.

Arthur's Seat and Duddingston

Edinburgh is blessed with many magnificent green, open spaces, and none better than Holyrood Park – or Queen's Park – a 650-acre wilderness of mountains, crags, lochs, moorland, marshes, fields and glens – all within walking distance of the city centre. This is one of the city's greatest assets, and it's easy to wander around till you're lost from the eyes and ears of civilization. The park's main feature, and the city's main landmark, is the 823 ft-high (237m) **Arthur's Seat***, the igneous core of another extinct volcano, and the highest of Edinburgh's hills. It is a genuine bit of wilderness right in the centre of Scotland's capital, and one climbed regularly by the city's residents. Another dominating feature of the Edinburgh skyline is the precipitous* **Salisbury Crags***, lying directly opposite the south gates of Holyrood Palace.*

 ▸▸ *See Eating and drinking p151, Sports p214*

◉ Sights

★ Walking up Arthur's Seat

For a map of the various routes, along with timings, visit the
Holyrood Park Information Centre, opposite Holyrood Palace,
T/F 556 1761, hsrangers@scotland.gov.uk *Map 5, A7, p255*

The best walk in Edinburgh is to the summit of Arthur's Seat, from
where you get the best view of the city, as well as the Pentland Hills
to the south, the Firth of Forth and Fife to the north, and, on a clear
day, to the Highland peaks, 70 or 80 miles away. The walk to the top
is a popular one so, if you want to avoid the crowds during summer,
make an early start. You'll need strong footwear, especially if it's wet,
and waterproofs, as there is little shelter in the park.

There are several different routes. The easiest way is to drive to
Dunsapie Loch and walk straight up to the top. Another route
starts from the car park on Queen's Drive, beside Holyrood Palace,
and follows the Radical Road along the foot of Salisbury Crags. The
track passes **Hutton's Rock**, a monolith named after James Hutton
(1726-97), the father of modern geology, whose theories, based on
studies of igneous rocks like the ones found at Salisbury Crags, are
the basis of our understanding of how the Earth was formed. A few
hundred yards further on a path leads uphill to the summit.

Duddingston Village

Map 5, p255

To all intents and purposes Duddingston is part of Edinburgh, but
more than any other 'village' it has managed to retain something
of its bucolic feel. It dates from the 12th century at least and was,

! The Radical Road is so called because it was built by a group
of labourers, hired by a committee headed by Sir Walter Scott,
who had been sacked for their radical political beliefs.

Macabre miniatures

Arthur's Seat was the scene of a bizarre find in 1836 when 17 miniature coffins were unearthed, each containing a tiny clothed figure. No one knows why or by whom they were buried, but at the time of the discovery *The Scotsman* newspaper suggested they were used by witches casting death spells on their enemies. Another theory was that they were kept by sailors to protect against death, and yet another that they represented a mock burial for the 17 victims of Burke and Hare (see p55). The story of the tiny coffins has fired the imagination of crime writer, Ian Rankin, and some of them can be seen at the Museum of Scotland.

until the early 20th century, very much separate from its large neighbour. **Duddingston Loch**, to the south of the village kirk, is famous as the scene of Sir Henry Raeburn's renowned painting of the *Reverend Robert Walker Skating on Duddingston Loch*, which is one display at the National Gallery (see p72). On the shores of Duddingston Loch is Thomson's Tower, an octagonal building designed in 1823 by William Playfair for the Duddingston Loch Curling Society. When the loch froze over curling was played here and in 1715 the society was formed. It was to curling what the Royal and Ancient is to golf: it standardized the rules of the game. The society still exists, though it hasn't played for many years. Its motto reads, in true Scottish modesty: "This is the way the Scots play: the rest of the world isn't half so lucky." Which obviously inspired Britain's Olympic curlers in Salt Lake City in 2002. Directly opposite the gates to the church is The Causeway, which leads you to the venerable old Sheep Heid Inn (see p151).

! According to legend, if you wash your face in the dew at the top of Arthur's Seat on May Day you'll stay young forever.

You can follow the path round to the south shore of the loch, to the entrance of the **Bawsinch Nature Reserve and Duddingston Loch Bird Sanctuary**, which is home to many bird species, including mute and whooper swans, short-eared owl and great spotted woodpecker. Note, though, that the path is intermittent and very muddy in places. Running along the southern boundary of the Bird Sanctuary is the **Innocent Railway** line, now a walkway and cycle path. The railway (which gets its name from the fact that carriages were first pulled by horses, a reference to the "innocent" means of transport) was built in 1831 to carry coal from the pits around Dalkeith to the goods yard at St Leonards and closed in 1968. You can return to Holyrood Palace car park via the Innocent Railway by following Duddingston Road west from the foot of Jacob's Ladder. The road runs along the side of the loch, giving a great view of **Samson's Ribs** rising steeply to the right.

New Town

The neoclassical New Town, one of the boldest schemes of civic architecture in the history of Europe, is what makes Edinburgh a truly world-class city, every bit as impressive as Paris or Prague, Rome or Vienna. Built in a great burst of creativity between 1767 and 1840, it is still inconceivable how, in the words of one historian, "a small, crowded, almost medieval town, the capital of a comparatively poor country, expanded in a short space of time, without foreign advice or foreign assistance, so as to become one of the enduringly beautiful cities of western Europe". Aside from its architectural kudos, the New Town is also the place in the city to eat, drink and be fashionable, especially along the main thoroughfare, George Street.

▸▸ *See Sleeping p124, Eating and drinking p151, Bars and clubs p175*

◉ Sights

Princes Street
Map 2, D1-C5, p248

The southernmost terrace of the New Town plan was never intended to be the most important, but Princes Street has developed into the city's main thoroughfare and principal shopping street. It is also one of the most visually spectacular streets in the world, because the south side has remained undeveloped, allowing superb uninterrupted views of the Castle Rock, across the valley now occupied by Princes Street Gardens. The north side of the street has lost any semblance of style and is now an undistinguished jumble of modern architecture, with a few notable exceptions. One is **Register House** (see below) and the other, opposite the Scott Monument, is the elegant 19th-century department store, **Jenners**, see Shopping, p205. At the east end of Princes Street is the St James Centre, a huge modern shopping complex that rears its ugly head behind Register House and serves as an unhappy testament to the city's single greatest planning blunder. Directly opposite is North Bridge, built originally in the 1760s as the main artery between the Old and New Towns and completely rebuilt in the late 19th century to span Waverley Station. On one corner is the Balmoral Hotel, one of the most luxurious of the city's hotels and a major landmark. Beside the hotel, the Waverley Market is a tasteful modern shopping complex, sunk discreetly below street level, and in stark contrast to the St James Centre.

General Register House and New Register House

T 334 0380, **F** 314 4400, www.gro-scotland.gov.uk *Mon-Fri 0900-1630. Map 2, C5, p248*

The General Register House (1774-1834) is one of Adam's most sumptuous and glorious buildings, and behind it is New Register House, the headquarters of the Scottish Record Office, which stores historical and legal documents – including birth, marriage and death certificates, wills and census records – dating as far back as the mid-16th century. Those wishing to trace their family roots should start here. It costs £17 for a day's search and, as there are limited places available, it's advisable to book in advance. A half-day search (after 1300) is £10 but can't be booked.

Scott Monument

Princes St Gardens East, **T** 529 4068. *1 Apr-30 Sep Mon-Sat 0900-1800, Sun 1000-1800; 1 Oct-31 Mar Mon-Sat 0900-1500, Sun 1000-1500. £2.50. Map 2, D3, p248*

Running along most of the south side of Princes Street are the sunken Princes Street Gardens, formed by the draining of Nor' Loch in the 1760s and now a very pleasant place to sit and relax during the summer. Standing in East Princes Street Gardens is the toweing Scott Monument, over 200 ft high and resembling a huge Gothic spaceship, built in 1844 as a fitting tribute to one of Scotland's greatest literary figures, who lived at 39 North Castle Street. The monument, the largest in the world in honour of an author, was designed by a self-taught architect called George Meikle Kemp, who tragically drowned in a canal shortly before the monument was completed. Beneath the archway is a statue of Sir Walter Scott, and there are also 64 statuettes of characters from his novels. The monument is open to the public, and a 287-step staircase climbs to a platform near the top of the spire, from where you get wonderful views.

★ National Gallery of Scotland and Royal Scottish Academy

The Mound, **T** 624 6200, www.nationalgalleries.org *Daily 1000-1700, Thu till 1900. Free (charge made for special loan exhibitions). Wheelchair access, lifts. For details of the disabled bus service to various arts venues, see p227. A free shuttle bus runs between the city's major galleries, see p24. Map 2, D2, p248*

At the junction of The Mound and Princes Street are two of Edinburgh's most impressive neoclassical public buildings, the Royal Scottish Academy and the National Gallery of Scotland, both designed by William Playfair between 1822 and 1845 in the style of Greek temples.

The National Gallery houses the most important collection of Old Masters in the UK outside London and boasts many masterpieces from almost every period in Western art and, though it may not be on the same massive scale as the National Gallery in London or the Louvre, it has the advantage of being more manageable and accessible. Begun originally by the old Royal Institution in the 1830s, the collection was given international credibility in 1946 by the loan of the Duke of Sutherland's collection, one of the finest in the UK, including major works by Titian, Raphael and Rembrandt and renowned Scottish painters such as Ramsay, Raeburn and Wilkie. The original Playfair rooms on the ground floor were restored to their 1840s appearance a few years ago, with the pictures hung closely together, often on two levels, and interspersed with various sculptures and objets d'art. The whole effect is somehow homely and altogether human. The layout is more or less chronological, starting in the upper rooms above the entrance and continuing clockwise around the ground floor. The rear section of the upper floor often has temporary exhibitions and the basement or lower floor contains most of the Scottish Collection.

● *If you visit the gallery in January you have the rare opportunity to see its excellent collection of Turner watercolours.*

The National Gallery's neighbour, the **Royal Academy**, was built to house the Society of Antiquaries and the Royal Society. In 1911 it was converted into the headquarters of the Royal Scottish Academy and is now used as a temporary exhibition space. It also acts as an overspill during the Festival when the National Gallery stages much larger exhibitions. At the time of going to press, the RSA is closed for refurbishment as part of the £26 million Playfair Project. It is due to reopen in August 2003 when it will stage a major Monet exhibition. Work is also well underway on the other part of the Playfair Project, an undergound link between the two galleries which will include a lecture theatre, shop and restaurant. This is due for completion in 2005.

Princes Street Gardens West
Map 4, B11/12, p253

On the other side of The Mound is West Princes Street Gardens, beautifully located right under the steep sides of Castle Rock. At the entrance is the world's oldest Floral Clock, which is laid out every year with over 20,000 plants. Further west is the Wellhouse Tower, one of the oldest buildings in the city, dating from the reign of David II (1329-71). At the far western corner of Princes Street Gardens, below the junction of Princes Street and Lothian Road, is **St Cuthbert's Church** and churchyard. This is the oldest church site in the city, dating back to the reign of Malcolm III, though the present church was mostly built in the 1890s. The churchyard is worth visiting and a peaceful refuge from the Princes Street traffic. Here lies the latter-day Irvine Welsh, Thomas de Quincey (1785-1859), author of *Confessions of an English Opium Eater*, a classic account of drug addiction in the early 19th century. De Quincey spent the last years of his life in Edinburgh. Close by, on the corner of Princes Street and Lothian Road, is the very attractive **St John's Church**, designed in 1818 by William Burn. The interior, modelled on St George's Chapel at Windsor Castle, is worth a look.

● *The Cornerstone Café beneath St John's Church is a good place for a cheap vegetarian lunch.*

St Andrew Square
Map 2, B3/4, p248

At the eastern end of George Street is St Andrew Square, which began life as a fashionable residential area but is now home to the headquarters of banks, building societies and insurance companies. The most impressive building, on the eastern side of the square, is the headquarters of **The Royal Bank of Scotland**. This handsome 18th-century town house was originally the home of Sir Laurence Dundas, but was remodelled in the 1850s when the wonderful domed ceiling was added. In the centre of the square is a massive 100-ft pillar carrying the statue of the lawyer and statesman Henry Dundas, first Viscount Melville (1742-1811), once described as the "absolute dictator of Scotland". Fashion has returned to the square in the shape of **Harvey Nichols**, the top Knightsbridge department store (see p205). Beside the store is The Walk, an alleyway leading to the St James shopping centre lined with exclusive fashion retail outlets, which have yet to open at the time of going to press. The shiny new bus station (see p22) can also be accessed, via an escalator, from St Andrew Square.

George Street
Map 2, C1-B3, p248 See also Shopping p204

To the north of Princes Street, and running parallel to it, is once venerable George Street, which has made the move from finance to fashion. If Carrie and Co from 'Sex and the City' lived in Edinburgh this is where they'd spend their Saturdays, maxing their credit cards in style. Those who prefer not to worship false gods can seek refuge in the **Church of St Andrew and St George**. The church is famous as the scene of the "Great Disruption" of

Great Scott
Tributes to Sir Walter Scott are everywhere, but none are more impressive than the Scott Monument in Princes Street Gardens.

1843, when the Church of Scotland was split in two. Further along are the **Assembly Rooms and Music Hall** (1787), once the social hub of the New Town and now a major Fringe venue.

Charlotte Square
Map 4, A10/11, p253

At the western end of the street is Charlotte Square, designed by Robert Adam in 1791 and considered by most to be his masterpiece. Like its counterpart, St Andrew Square, Charlotte Square was originally purely residential, but is now the heart of the city's financial community. Charlotte Square has long been the most prestigious address in the city, particularly the north side, the oldest part and the best preserved. **Number six** is the official residence of the Secretary of State for Scotland, and the upper floors of **number seven** are the official residence of the Moderator of the General Assembly of the Church of Scotland. On the west side of the square is St George's Church, originally designed by Adam but, following his death in 1792, the plans were abandoned on grounds of cost and the building you see today was built in 1811 by Robert Reid. In the 1960s it was refurbished as West Register House (part of the Scottish Record Office), which is open to the public and features displays of historical documents (*Mon-Fri 1000-1600, free*). Numbers 26-31 on the south side of the square, have undergone a major conservation repair programme undertaken by the National Trust for Scotland (NTS) and their façade has been returned to its original condition. No 28 has become the headquarters of the National Trust for Scotland and incorporates a fine café.

Georgian House

7 Charlotte Sq, **T** 226 3318. *1 Apr-31 Oct daily 1000-1700; 1 Nov-31 Mar daily 1100-1500. Adults £5, concessions £3.75. Map 4, A10, p253*

The lower floors of number seven are open to the public as the Georgian House, which gives a fascinating insight into how Edinburgh's gentry lived in the late 18th century. The house has been lovingly restored by the National Trust for Scotland and is crammed with period furniture and hung with fine paintings, including portraits by Ramsay and Raeburn.

Queen Street

Map 2, B1-A3

Parallel to George Street, and slightly downhill from it, is Queen Street, the most northerly terrace of James Craig's New Town plan, bordered by Queen Street Gardens to the north. This was a prime residential area of the New Town, with excellent views across the Firth of Forth to Fife. The air of exclusivity is maintained in that the gardens are accessible only to key holders who live nearby.

● *On the north side of Queen Street Gardens is Heriot Row, where Robert Louis Stevenson spent most of his life (at number 17).*

Moray Estate
Map 3, H4, p250

The earliest of the New Town extensions, begun in 1803, was the Northern New Town, which extends downhill from Queen Street Gardens as far as Fettes Row to the north. This area is the best preserved of the New Town extensions and has retained its residential character. The latest, and finest, part of the northern development, begun in 1822, is the Moray Estate, to the east of Queensferry Street, designed by James Gillespie Graham, another of Edinburgh's architectural geniuses. This part of the New Town is characterized by gracious curves and circles, none finer than Moray Place, a magnificent twelve-sided circus with a circular central garden surrounded by grand and rather imposing four-storey houses. Northwest from here, cobbled streets run downhill to Stockbridge.

★ Scottish National Portrait Gallery
Queen St, **T** 624 6200, www.nationalgalleries.org *Daily 1000-1700, Thu till 1900. Free. Photography collection open to visitors by prior appointment only:* **T** 624 6405. *Map 2, A3, p248*

At the far eastern end of Queen street is this phenomenal collection of the great and the good (and the bad and the ugly) of Scottish history. The building itself is a fantastical French Gothic medieval palace in red sandstone, modelled on the Doge's Palace in Venice. The stunning foyer is decorated with William Hole's wonderful frieze of famous Scots, as well as paintings depicting two of the most important events in Scottish history, the Battle of Bannockburn and the Battle of Largs. The gallery's displays start chronologically on the top floor, where you'll find Scotland's two most tragic and romantic characters, Mary, Queen of Scots and a young Bonnie Prince Charlie; Robert Burns painted by his friend, Alexander Nasmyth; Sir Walter Scott by Raeburn; David Hume the philosopher; James Watt the engineer; and Robert Louis Stevenson. Though the subjects are, by definition, more important and well-known than the artists, there are nevertheless some mighty fine painters represented here, such as Van Dyck, Gainsborough, Raeburn and Kokoschka. The top floor of the gallery runs to the end of the 19th century, and the middle floor takes us through from Edwardian times to the present day, with artists including Compton Mackenzie (Whisky Galore), poet and socialist Hugh McDiarmid; film director Bill Forsyth; writer Muriel Spark; fashion designer Jean Muir; actor Sean Connery and writer Irvine Welsh. The gallery houses the **National Collection of Photography**, with regular photographic exhibitions held throughout the year on the ground floor. The print room and archives contain a valuable collection of photographs of famous Scots as well as the social history index. There's also a shop and a good café on the ground floor.

Calton Hill and Broughton

*In the first few decades of the 19th century there were major extensions to the original New Town, spreading to the north, west and east, and all in keeping with the neoclassical theme. Perhaps the most interesting of these extensions is the area around **Calton Hill**, another of Edinburgh's extinct volcanoes, which grew beyond the east end of Princes Street. The slopes of Calton Hill are covered with many fine buildings and it is probably these which earned Edinburgh the sobriquet 'Athens of the North'. The eastern New Town is bordered by*

Broughton Street, *heart of the city's gay scene and home to many of its hippest bars and clubs.*

▸▸ *See Sleeping p127, Eating and drinking p157, Bars and clubs p177, Gay and lesbian p215*

Sights

★ Calton Hill
Map 2, p249

Calton Hill is well worth climbing for some of the best views in the city. From the top, Arthur's Seat and Salisbury Crags seem so close you could almost reach out and touch them, and you can see the Pentland Hills to the south, along the Lothian coast to Berwick Law and across the bridges to Fife. The whole effect is astounding, especially the view up Princes Street to the Castle. The quickest route to the top starts from the east end of Princes Street, at the corner of North Bridge and Waterloo Place. Head up the north side of Waterloo Place, past the turning into Calton Hill on the left, and follow the steps, signposted Calton Hill, up to the left and then immediately right.

The monuments at the top of Calton Hill are also worth the climb. They form the four corners of a precinct and make for a strange collection. Most famous is the **National Monument**, built to commemorate the Scots who died in the Napoleonic Wars. The architect, Charles Robert Cockerell (1788-1863) intended it to be an imitation of the Parthenon in Athens and chose as his assistant the young William Playfair, who went on to design some of the city's most notable imitations of Classical Greek architecture, such as the National Gallery of Scotland (see p72). The project was carried out on a massive scale and, not surprisingly, in 1822, three years after it had begun, the £24,000 raised for the project ran out with only 12 columns built. However, this was in keeping with the

It's all Greek to me
The National Monument, derided as a national disgrace at the time, inspired the city's architects to design the 'Athens of the North'.

original contract drawing, so what we see today was the architect's intention – a deliberate folly. Though it caused much controversy and was labelled 'Scotland's disgrace', it did serve to inspire all subsequent building in the 'Athens of the North'.

On the west side of the hill, overlooking the St James Centre, is the old **Calton Hill Observatory**, also built by Playfair in 1818. It was abandoned in 1894 when light pollution became too great, and relocated to Blackford Hill (see p97). The observatory building was bought by the city council and renamed the City Observatory. Since 1953 it has been home to the Astronomical Society of Edinburgh. It is open most Friday nights, if the skies are clear enough, and visitors with an interest in astronomy are welcome (www.astronomyedinburgh.org). An earlier building was planned by James Craig, first architect of the New Town, but the money ran out and all that remains is castle-like Observatory House.

Southwest of the observatory is the **Monument to Dugald Stewart** (1753-1828), a Playfair construction commemorating an obscure University professor. Completing the quartet of monuments is **Nelson's Monument** (*Apr-Sep Mon 1300-1800, Tue-Sat 1000-1800; Oct-Mar Mon-Sat 1000-1500. £2.50*), a 108-ft tower in the shape of an upturned telescope, built in 1816 to celebrate Nelson's victory at the Battle of Trafalgar. It's worth climbing to the top of the monument, for the panoramic views are even better. In the mid-19th century the Astronomer Royal for Scotland introduced a time signal for sailors at Leith. The five foot diameter ball still drops from the crossbars at the top of the Nelson Monument at precisely 1300 every day.

● *Calton Hill is the site of anarchic pagan festivities at the feast of Beltane in May, see p197, and at night it's a popular cruising area for the nearby gay community.*

Royal High School and Regent Terrace
Map 2, C9, p249

On the southern slopes of Calton Hill, on Regent Road, is the old Royal High School, designed in 1829 by former pupil Thomas Hamilton. Designed integrally with the National Monument on Calton Hill to create an Edinburgh Acropolis, the Royal High School building is considered the finest Greek Revival building in Scotland and perhaps the one building which most justified the city's nickname. The Royal High is the oldest school in Scotland, dating back to the 12th century (the previous premises were near the Cowgate in the Old Town), and its long list of famous former pupils includes Robert Adam, Sir Walter Scott and Alexander Graham Bell. The school was moved in 1970 to the western outskirts of the city. The building had been proposed as the seat of the new Parliament when devolution of government for Scotland first seemed a reality back in the mid-1970s, but following the unsatisfactory referendum result plans were shelved. The building is now the Scottish HQ of the Crown Office. Almost opposite the former High School is the **Burns Monument**, erected in 1830 as a tribute to Scotland's greatest poet, who died aged only 37. Beyond the old Royal High School building is **Regent Terrace**, a particularly fine example of the city's New Town architecture, with its Doric porticoes and trellis

★ **City views**

Best
- From the Castle across the New Town, p33
- From the Forth Floor restaurant across the Firth of Forth, p153
- From the top of Arthur's Seat, p67
- From Calton Hill down the length of Princes Street, p78

balconies, designed by William Playfair in 1825. Regent Terrace leads into Carlton Terrace which curves round into **Royal Terrace**, a magnificent row of 40 houses.

St Andrew's House and Old Calton Burial Ground
Map 2, C8, p249

On the south side of Regent Road is St Andrew's House, a massive art deco structure housing government offices, built on the site of Calton Jail. Until 1864, public executions were carried out on top of the jail, watched by crowds who stood to the south of the City Observatory. The only part of the jail that remains is the castellated Governor's House, which looks on to the Old Calton Burial Ground. The cemetery contains Robert Adam's tower built for the great empiricist David Hume, Thomas Hamilton's obelisk to the political martyrs of 1793, and a memorial to the Scottish-American soldiers who fought in the American Civil War, complete with a statue of Abraham Lincoln. You may come across a mausoleum to Robert Burns, but this is for the architect of the Nelson Monument (see above) and not to be confused with the poet Robert Burns.

Broughton Street
Map 3, G9-F8, p251

Broughton Street and the streets around it form Edinburgh's so-called 'pink triangle', heart of the city's thriving gay scene.

With an atmosphere redolent of New York's East Village, Broughton Street is home to many of the city's hippest bars, clubs, cafés and restaurants. On the corner of Broughton Street and East London Street is **Mansfield Place Church**, a late 19th-century neo Norman edifice, now famous as the site of Pre-Raphaelite murals by Phoebe Traquair, a leading light in the Scottish Arts and Crafts Movement. These murals were created by her over eight years (1893-1901), working alone seven days a week without pay, but they have suffered badly due to years of neglect. The church has been turned into offices but the murals are being restored for public display. Her work can also be seen on the walls of the Song School at St Mary's Cathedral (see p87). At the top of Leith Walk, next to the Playhouse Theatre, is the new Omni Complex which opens in May 2003 and houses bars, restaurants, a cinema, hotel (see p127) and comedy club (see p189).

● *In the centre of the roundabout at the top of Leith Walk is the statue of Sherlock Holmes, the world's most famous fictional detective. His creator, Arthur Conan Doyle, was born at 11 Picardy Place in 1859.*

Stockbridge and Inverleith

Over the years, Edinburgh's New Town spread out beyond its original plan to swallow up a series of quaint little villages. One of these, the once bohemian Stockbridge, is the perfect antidote to all that perfect symmetry and neoclassical grandeur. Stockbridge has been home to many artists and writers over the years, among them the painter Sir Henry Raeburn (1756-1823) and 19th-century junkie Thomas de Quincey (1785-1859), author of Confessions of an English Opium Eater *(see also p73). Though Stockbridge has all but lost its rakish charm, it remains one of Edinburgh's most beguiling corners and is an interesting place to explore with its jumble of antique shops and second-hand bookstores.*

▶▶ *See Sleeping p129, Eating and drinking p158, Bars and clubs p179*

◉ Sights

Around Stockbridge
Map 3, p250

Start in St Stephen Street, which is lined with antique and junk shops and a great place to spend an hour or two browsing (see Shopping, p201). Follow St Stephen Street as it curves round to the right and at the end is the massive St Stephen's Church, designed by Playfair and built in 1828. From here, turn left up West Silvermills Lane to reach Henderson Row, where you'll find the neoclassical **Edinburgh Academy**, which was used in 1968 as the model for Marcia Blaine's School for Girls in the screen adaptation of Muriel Spark's *Prime of Miss Jean Brodie* (see p237). Head back west along Henderson Row, which becomes Hamilton Place and leads in turn along the south bank of the Water of Leith to the Stock Bridge which crosses the Water of Leith. The original bridge was built in 1786 but the one you see today dates from 1900. Across the other side of the bridge are several fine restaurants, making this a good point to stop for lunch.

The residential streets on the far side of the river were developed by the painter Henry Raeburn. Head left along Dean Terrace to reach the most notable of these, **Ann Street**, named after his wife and described by the poet Sir John Betjeman as "the most attractive street in Britain". It is now one of the most expensive addresses in the city and the only street in the New Town whose houses each have a front garden. Nearby **Danube Street** was once home to Edinburgh's most notorious brothel, run until the 1980s by Nora Doyce, who described it as a 'YMCA with extras'.

Green belter
The Royal Botanic Garden is the perfect place for a picnic on those rare warm summer days.

★ Royal Botanic Garden
T 552 7171. *Daily 1000-1600 Nov-Feb; till 1800 Mar-Apr and Sep-Oct; till 2000 May-Aug. Free, but voluntary donations welcomed. There are two entrances; the West Gate, on Arboretum Place, and East Gate on Inverleith Row. Buses 8, 17, 23 and 27 from the city centre. Map 3, p250 See also Kids p224*

North of Stockbridge is the district of Inverleith, where you'll find Edinburgh's gorgeous Royal Botanic Garden. Contained within its 72 acres is a mind-boggling variety of plants and trees, as well as walkways, ornamental gardens, various hothouses and huge open spaces. Many of the exotic species you can see were discovered by Scottish collectors during their expeditions around the globe. There's an awful lot to enjoy, but particularly notable are the outdoor rock garden, the huge Victorian Palm House, the Glasshouse Experience and the new Chinese Garden, featuring the largest collection of Chinese wild plants outside China. Near the West Gate, at the highest point in the Garden, is **Inverleith House**, a fine Georgian mansion which used to house the Scottish National Gallery of Modern Art. It now stages a changing programme of exhibitions. There's a shop at the West Gate selling gifts, books and cards, and a snack bar near the West Gate. A leaflet which has a map of the Garden is on sale at both gates.

● *Next to Inverleith House is the Terrace Café (see p159), a great place for lunch or a snack, or just to sit with a coffee and admire the stupendous views from across the New Town to the Castle.*

West Edinburgh

Stretching from Princes Street and Lothian Road out towards the city bypass and the airport is West Edinburgh, an indefinable sprawl of mostly residential streets, which on the surface appears to offer little to visitors. This part of the city was once its main engine room, with dozens of breweries and the water-borne trade from the Union Canal. The old industries have mostly disappeared and the area around Lothian Road and the West Approach Road, called The Exchange, has reinvented itself as Edinburgh's new financial district. At the west end of Princes Street is the start of Lothian Road, one of Edinburgh's busiest thoroughfares, which runs south to Tollcross. At weekends Lothian Road becomes a seething mass of drunken bodies pouring out from the many bars that line its route. Ironically, however, it is also very close to three of the city's main cultural venues: the Usher Hall, the Royal Lyceum Theatre and the Traverse Theatre (see p193). From Tollcross, Fountainbridge heads west towards the outlying districts of Gorgie and Slateford. On the way it passes the Fountain Brewery, one of only two breweries remaining in a city which once boasted more than 40. The brewery cannot be visited but its presence can certainly be recognized by the pungent yeasty whiff that permeates this part of Edinburgh for much of the time.

▸▸ *See Sleeping p131, Eating and drinking p160, Bars and clubs p180*

◉ Sights

West End to Dean Village
Map 4, p253

The western extension of the New Town followed a couple of years after the eastern extension and spread southwest from Shandwick Place, along West Maitland Street to Haymarket, whose railway station was built in 1840 as the original terminus of the line from Glasgow, before it was extended east to Waverley. The New Town also spread northwest along Queensferry Street towards Melville Street, the most impressive thoroughfare in the West End. At its western end in Palmerston Place is **St Mary's Cathedral**, the second largest church in Scotland, designed by George Gilbert Scott in Gothic style, and featuring a set of murals by Phoebe Traquair (see p83).

Queensferry Street, which heads west out of the city towards the Forth Rail and Road Bridges (see p107), crosses the steep valley of the Water of Leith along the 100-ft-high **Dean Bridge**. Below the bridge is Dean Village, a quaint former milling village straddling the Water of Leith, once separate from the city, and now a quiet refuge from the West End traffic. At the north end of Dean Bridge, to the west of Trinity Church, is **Dean Cemetery**, one of Edinburgh's finest last resting places. The cemetery houses the graves of the likes of architect William Playfair, pioneering photographer Octavius Hill, and Dr Joseph Bell, who is said to have been the flesh-and-blood inspiration for Arthur Conan Doyle's character Sherlock Holmes. It also contains many excellent examples of 19th-century sculpture.

★ Scottish National Gallery of Modern Art

Belford Rd, **T** 624 6200, **F** 343 3250, www.nationalgalleries.org
*Daily 1000-1700, Thu till 1900. Free. The gallery is a 10-min taxi ride
from the city centre, 15-mins walk from Haymarket station, or bus 13
from George St to Belford Rd. For details of the Galleries Bus which
travels between this gallery, the Dean Gallery, the National Gallery
and the National Portrait Gallery, see p24. Map 4, A6, p252*

About 10 minutes' walk from Dean Village along the Water of Leith
Walkway (see p90) is the Scottish National Gallery of Modern Art,
the first ever gallery in Britain devoted to 20th-century art when it
opened to the public in 1984. The permanent collection features
everything from the Impressionists to Hockney and, though it may
be dwarfed by the likes of London's Tate Modern, a few hours
spent wandering round this brilliant collection is an extremely
rewarding and thoroughly enjoyable experience. It is particularly
strong on Expressionism, with works by Picasso, Cézanne, Matisse,
Magritte, Mondrian, Henry Moore, Kandinsky, Klee, Giacometti and
Sickert all displayed, among many other important names, including many contemporary Scottish artists. There are also frequent
temporary exhibitions, and don't miss the excellent café, especially
if the sun is shining (see p162).

The gallery is housed in the former John Watson's School, a
neoclassical building designed by William Burn in 1825, and the
spacious grounds are dotted with sculptures by Paolozzi, Henry
Moore and Dan Graham. The gallery makes the ideal day out,
especially when combined with its sister gallery, the Dean, across
the other side of the road (see below), and a walk along the Water
of Leith. Though weak on new Scottish artists, the downstairs
galleries feature a strong collection of 20th-century Scottish painters, particularly the so-called **Glasgow Boys** – Steven Campbell,
Peter Howson, Ken Currie and Adrian Wiszniewski – as well as the
Colourists – Peploe, Cadell, Hunter and Fergusson.

Revival of the finest

The New Town's neoclassical architecture is unparalleled in Britain.

The upstairs galleries feature international art and the big names from Fauvism, Surrealism, Abstract Expressionism and Cubism, including George Braque and Picasso, Henry Matisse, a number of works by René Magritte, Joan Miró, Max Ernst, Duchamp and Giacometti and Pollock. Alongside these are the British greats like Francis Bacon, Helen Chadwick and Damien Hirst. The permanent collections are augmented by temporary exhibitions, details of which can be found in the free monthly Edinburgh Gallery Guide.

Dean Gallery
Belford Rd. *Same opening hours as the Gallery of Modern Art. Café open Mon-Sat 1000-1630, Sun 1400-1630.* Map 4, A7, p253

Standing opposite the National Gallery of Modern Art, the Dean houses the Gift of Edinburgh-born sculptor, **Sir Eduardo Paolozzi**, which comprises his sculptures, graphic art and a recreation of his studio. But more than being just a shrine to the work of Paolozzi, the gallery also features one of the most complete collections of Dada and Surrealist art in Britain, acquired from the collections of Sir Roland Penrose and marmalade heiress Gabrielle Keillor. It includes all the main players of Surrealism: Dali, Ernst, Magritte, Miró, Man Ray, Tanguy, Delvaux and, of course, the great man himself, Picasso. The Dean also houses a large library and archive of books, manuscripts and correspondence from the Dada and Surrealist movements, as well as exhibitions of contemporary art, a shop and café. Though not as wide-ranging as its near-neighbour, the Dean is a surreal treat for modern art lovers.

★ Water of Leith
Visitor Centre, 24 Lanark Rd, **T** 455 7367, www.waterofleith. edin.org *Bus 44, 44A. Apr-Sep daily 1000-1600; Nov-Mar Wed-Sun 1000-1600. Adults £1.90, concessions £1.20, family £5. Bus 28 or 35 from Fountainbridge, see p93.*

If the weather's fair, one of the finest pleasures this city has to offer is the walk along the bucolic Water of Leith. The Water of Leith Walkway follows the small river from Balerno, on the western outskirts of the city, all the way to the docks at Leith – a distance of 11¼ miles (19 km). The section described here covers the most beautiful stretch, the few miles from the Scottish National Gallery of Modern Art and Dean Gallery to the Royal Botanic Garden.

Starting from Belford Bridge, the path follows the Water of Leith as it slides gently through a peaceful, wooded valley. The river tumbles over a weir past a new housing development and then takes you into **Dean Village**, one of the oldest parts of the city and one of its most charismatic little crannies. Beyond Dean Village the walkway passes below the high-arched Dean Bridge, built in 1832 and designed by the great Scottish civil engineer Thomas Telford. About 500 yards further along is **St Bernard's Well**, an early 19th-century mineral spring that was thought to have health-giving properties. The Doric 'temple' on top was designed and built in 1789 by the painter and architect Alexander Naysmyth, a good friend of Robert Burns. Soon after, the path heads into **Stockbridge**, where there are plenty of good pubs, cafés and restaurants. The path continues at the foot of the steps, which lead down from Pizza Express, and after a few hundred yards stops at the next bridge. Here you have to return to street level and turn left, then immediately right on to Arboretum Avenue. On the right across the river you'll see rows of attractive little two-storey terraced houses known as The Colonies. Follow Arboretum Avenue as it heads up to a road junction, then cross the road and walk up Arboretum Road to the west gate of the **Botanic Gardens** (see p85). Leaving the Gardens by the east gate, on Inverleith Row, you can easily rejoin the Walkway and continue all the way to Leith.

● *Cross the road outside the gate and turn right. Here, at No 8 Howard Place, is where Robert Louis Stevenson was born in November 1850.*

The Exchange
Map 4, C10/11, p253

The triangle formed by Lothian Road, the West Approach Road and Morrison Street, now known as The Exchange, is Edinburgh's new 'International Financial Centre', which basically consists of the starkly functional bulk of the Sheraton Grand Hotel, the ambitious **Edinburgh International Conference Centre**, designed by Terry Farrell and opened in 1995, Baillie Gifford's Rutland Court, the Clydesdale Bank Plaza, the Standard Life building and the truly innovative new headquarters of Scottish Widows. In stark contrast to the understated 'old money' of the neighbouring West End, The Exchange is notable for its brash, ostentatious wealth – a huge concrete and steel temple to Mammon, where drones and workers emerge at lunchtime to make calls on their 3G phones and have a smoke or a coffee in one of those ubiquitous chains. Those above them in the food chain sit in the sleek, chic Santini restaurant (see p161) or perhaps pop into the fabulous new One health spa (see p212) to work on those abs or work off some executive stress after a tough day at the stock-face.

Union Canal
Map 4, p253

Lothian Road continues south to Fountainbridge, which heads west to the point where the Union Canal now ends. Completed in 1822, the canal ran all the way to Falkirk, where it linked up with the Forth and Clyde Canal to Glasgow. Now, with the opening of the Falkirk Wheel, as part of the ambitious Millennium Link project, the Union and Forth and Clyde Canals have been revived and a continuous waterway between Edinburgh and Glasgow re-opened. The best access on to the canal is via Gilmore Park. From here you can stroll along the towpath all the way to Slateford, where an aqueduct carries the canal over the Water of

Leith, but it's not the most attractive of walks. Steps lead down from the aqueduct to the Water of Leith Visitor Centre (see p90).

(see p90)

Shaping a Nation

Dundee St, **T** 229 0300, www.shaping-a-nation.co.uk *Mon 1430-2130, Tue-Thu 1200-1900, Fri-Sun 1200-2130. Adults £3.50, children and concessions £2. Turbo Venture not included in admission. Buses 1, 28, 34 and 35 stop outside Fountainpark. Map 4, E8, p253*

Fountainpark leisure complex is home to restaurants, bars, a gym, the huge Eros nightclub, a 13-screen cinema and Shaping a Nation, a tongue-in-cheek look at Scotland and the Scots' influence on the world. It may be a bit tacky for some, but provides a more irreverent approach and has lots of hands-on, interactive stuff to entertain even those with the most limited of attention spans. The main thrust is a long list of all the things invented by various McClever-Clogs: from penicillin to the gel-filled bra. You can even try cloning yourself à la Dolly the Sheep (may her DNA rest in peace). The most interesting feature is a push-button quiz called "So you think you ken Scotland?" Turbo Venture is a motion simulator with various rides, one of which flies you over mountains and glens in the Highlands and costs an extra £1.

Caledonian Brewery

42 Slateford Rd, www.caledonian-brewery.co.uk *1-hr tour costs £7 per person and includes beer sampling. Tours for groups of 10 or more can be arranged (at least 1 week in advance) through Caledonian Events, **T** 228 5688. Buses 4, 28, 35, 38 and 44 from the city centre. Map 4, G6, p252*

Just west of Fountainpark the road forks: right towards Tynecastle Park, home of Heart of Midlothian FC, and left towards the Caledonian Brewery, home of the very wonderful Caledonian 80/- and Deuchars IPA ales, which can be supped with extreme pleasure in the Caley Sample Room (see p180). The brewery also hosts regular ceilidhs and an annual beer festival. The Visitors Centre allows a fascinating insight into traditional brewing methods.

Edinburgh Zoo

T 334 9171, www.edinburghzoo.org.uk *Apr-Sep daily 0900-1800; Oct-Mar daily 0900-1630. Adults £7, children £4. Buses 12, 26/26A and 31 from Haymarket and Princes St. Penguin Parade at 1400 daily Mar-Oct, weather permitting. Map 1, p247 See also Kids, p223*

Three miles west of the city centre is Edinburgh's zoo, the largest in Scotland, set in 80 acres on the side of Corstorphine Hill. Whatever you think of zoos, this one is highly respected for its serious work, as well as being an enormous amount of fun. There are over 1,000 animals from all over the world, but the zoo is best known for its penguins – the largest breeding colony of Antarctic penguins anywhere outside Antarctica itself. The latest attractions are the endangered Asiatic lions and the Magic Forest, full of marmosets and tamarins. There are also animal-handling sessions, available at an extra £1 per person, and afternoon animal talks.

Lauriston Castle

Cramond Rd South, Davidson's Mains, **T** 336 2060. *Apr-Sep daily 0900-1800; Oct-Mar daily 0900-1700; Nov-Feb daily 0900-1630. Adults £7.50, concessions £5, children £4.50. Buses 16, 29 and 129 from Princes St. Map 1, p247*

About five miles northwest of the city centre is Lauriston Castle, a fine Edwardian country mansion set in lovely grounds overlooking the Firth of Forth. The original tower house is late 16th-century, with many neo-Jacobean additions by William Burn in the 19th century. It was once the home of John Law, founder of the first bank in France and obtained sole trading rights in the Lower Mississippi, which he christened Louisiana in honour of the French

King. The interior contains collections of period furniture and antiques. Lauriston is also the home of the Edinburgh Croquet Club.

Cramond

A local passenger ferry service crosses the River Almond at Cramond: 0900-1300 and 1400-1700 in summer, till 1600 in winter, closed Fri. Buses 41 and 42 from Hanover St. Map 1, p247

On the very edge of the city, where the River Almond flows into the Forth, is the little coastal village of Cramond. The 18th-century village of whitewashed houses is the site of an ancient Roman fort, a large part of which has been excavated. In addition to being steeped in ancient history, Cramond has a pleasant promenade, a golf course and a lovely, wooded walk along the banks of the Almond river towards the 16th-century **Old Cramond Brig**, where the Cramond Inn makes a fine spot for some liquid refreshment (see p180). And if that weren't enough to tempt you, there's also Cramond Island, which can be reached via a raised walkway when the tide is out. Just make sure you keep an eye on the time or you may find yourself stuck there for longer than you anticipated. Tide times are posted on the shore, and are also available from the tourist office (see p30).

South Edinburgh

*South of the Old Town is Edinburgh's **Southside**, home to the Univeristy's main campus. Beyond are Morningside to the west, Newington to the east and the Braid Hills to the south. This swathe of 19th-century middle-class housing is a comfortable mix of student flats – particularly in Marchmont and Newington – and genteel, blue-rinsed respectability. Here also are Bruntsfield and Mayfield, both choc-full of small hotels, guesthouses and B&Bs. There's little of real interest for visitors around this part of town, though **Blackford Hill** and **Hermitage of Braid** to the south are great places for a picnic or* *to blow away the cobwebs on a Sunday morning. However, the South comes into its own in the evenings, when the many bistros and restaurants attract hungry residents, and its bars fill with the large and thirsty local student population.*

▸▸ *See Sleeping p135, Eating and drinking p163, Bars and clubs p182*

 # Sights

Bruntsfield and The Meadows
Map 5, E1-4, p254

Immediately south of the University is The Meadows, a large area of parkland which is filled with impromptu football games on Sundays. It's a pleasant place to stroll or sit with a picnic on warm summer days, but not a safe place to walk alone at night. On the west side of The Meadows is Bruntsfield Links, which leads into the genteel 19th-century residential suburbs of Bruntsfield, Marchmont to the south and Merchiston to the southwest.

● *Bruntsfield is a good place to look for accommodation, as there are dozens of small hotels, guesthouses and B&Bs, as well as a good selection of restaurants.*

Morningside and Newington
Map 1, p247

Further south, beyond Merchiston, is Morningside, renowned for its distinctly posh accent, as heard in the film, *The Pride of Miss Jean Brodie*. Morningside is an area of "rifained zenzitivity", where the nearest thing you'll get to a drugs war is two old ladies fighting over a bottle of sanatogen in the local chemist shop. East of The Meadows is the residential suburb of Newington, handily placed for the Royal Commonwealth Pool and within easy striking distance of Arthur's Seat and Duddingston Village (see p67). Like

Bruntsfield, Newington is also full of guest houses, B&Bs and restaurants. East of Newington, on the other side of South Clerk Street, lies the insalubrious area of St Leonard's, home to Ian Rankin's fictional detective, Inspector John Rebus.

Craigmillar Castle

Craigmillar Castle Rd, off the Old Dalkeith Rd (A7), **T** 661 4445. *Apr-Sep daily 0930-1830; Oct-Mar Mon-Wed and Sat-Sun 1400-1630, Thu 0930-1230. Adults £2.20, concessions £1.60, children £0.75. Buses 2, 14, 21, 32 and 42 from the city centre and get off at the junction of Duddingston Rd West and Peffermill Rd. Map 1, p247*

Craigmillar Castle may be in ruins and roofless, but it is nonetheless an impressive and well-preserved example of a medieval Scots baronial castle, despite its proximity to a sprawling council estate. It dates from 1374, though the curtain wall was added in 1427. This failed to repel the Earl of Hertford's forces in 1544 during the 'Rough Wooing'. The castle was once a refuge for Mary, Queen of Scots, who came here in 1566 to grieve the murder of Rizzio at Holyrood, and it was also here that the murder of her husband, Lord Darnley, was plotted. The castle encompasses one and a half acres and there's plenty to be seen.

Braid Hills

Hermitage House, *Mon-Fri 1000-1600, Sun (Apr-Sep only) 1100-1800. Buses 11 and 15 from Princes St. Map 1, p247*

To the south of Marchmont are the Braid Hills, which are mostly occupied by two golf courses. The hills are ideal for a Sunday walk. The walk described here takes in the **Hermitage of Braid** and **Blackford Hill**, at the top of which stands the city's Royal Observatory. Start the walk from Braid Road, just off Comiston Road, which is the starting point for the Hermitage of Braid nature trail, a lovely gentle walk along the Braid Burn. The track is easy to follow

★ Walks in the city

and, although the hill is within the city, there's a real sense of being out in the countryside. The path takes you to Hermitage House, an 18th-century mansion which now serves as an information centre. From the Hermitage of Braid you can continue to the summit of Blackford Hill. Follow the main path which heads down the steep-sided, wooded glen, and cross the burn three times before reaching the end of the woods. Head up the steps to the left just after going under the wooden bridge, and keep on this path up to a point about 100 m ahead where a clear path heads to the right and climbs to join another path which takes you up to the Observatory. From here you can continue down towards Newington or retrace your steps back to Comiston Road and take a bus back to the city centre.

Royal Observatory

Blackford Hill, **T** 668 8405, www.roe.ac.uk *Mon-Sat 1000-1700, Sun 1200-1700. Adults £2.60, children and concessions £1.85, family £6. Bus 41 from The Mound and get off at Blackford Av, or walk from Comiston Rd via the Hermitage of Braid. Map 1, p247*

Though this isn't a working observatory, there are opportunities to look through the telescope on winter Friday evenings. The visitor centre is excellent and you can find out all about the mysteries of the solar system, play with various hands-on exhibits and enjoy the panoramic views of the city.

Leith, Newhaven and Portobello

*No part of Edinburgh has undergone such a dramatic transformation in recent years as Leith. One of Edinburgh's most depressed and roughest districts, Leith remained a separate burgh until as recently as the 1920s and even today likes to think of itself as distinct from the rest of the city. Like all British seaports, Leith's fortunes suffered during the postwar years with the decline in heavy industry, but since the mid-1980s Leith has been changed into one of the city's most fashionable areas. Old warehouses have been converted into expensive apartments, ad agencies, PR firms and civil servants moved in and the **Royal Yacht Britannia** settled into her new home at **Ocean Terminal**. The old port may have been gentrified, but it still has its rough edges, and you'll need to be careful after dark. Only a stone's throw from restaurants that can charge two weeks' dole money for a bottle of wine are grim, faceless council blocks, and many of its street corners are still filled with shivering prostitutes looking for business late at night. A mile west of Leith is the sleepy little port of Newhaven, which was once a separate village and, though it has now been swallowed up into the city, still has a different feel to it. To the east lies Portobello, erstwhile bathing resort for the city's well-to-do.*

▸▸ *Sleeping p138, Eating and drinking p165, Bars and clubs p183.*

 Sights

Around Leith

Buses 7, 10, 12, 16 and 22 from the top of Leith Walk (£0.80). A taxi costs around £4. Map 6, p256

The main focal point is **The Shore** which is lined with bars and restaurants. In the adjoining streets are some notable old buildings, such as **Lamb's House**, a well-preserved Renaissance house, which was the home of Andro Lamb, the merchant with whom

Mary, Queen of Scots spent her first night on her return to Scotland in 1561. Just east of the old Town Hall on Constitution Street is **Leith Links**, now a public park but which, it is claimed, was the world's first official golf course, in the 15th century. Back on The Shore is the acclaimed **Leith Gallery** (see p103).

Ocean Terminal

Ocean Dr, **T** 555 8888, **F** 555 3919, www.oceanterminal.com *Mon-Fri 1000-2000, Sat 0900-1900, Sun 1100-1800. Cinema, bars and restaurant open later. Free parking. Baby facilities. Wheelchairs and buggies available.* Map 6, A6, p256

This vast new shopping/entertainment complex is part of the push to re-launch Leith as a vibrant living and working district. Resembling an airport terminal from the outside and a cruise liner inside, it certainly looks good, but only time will tell if it manages to lure the crowds away from the city centre at the weekend. Most of the shops are of the standard High Street chain variety (Debenhams, BHS etc), but the ace up its sleeve is that the Royal Yacht Britannia is moored here and visible through the giant window that takes up the entire west side of the terminal. There are also cafés, bars and restaurants, including Terence Conran's Zinc Bar & Grill (see p167) and a 12-screen cinema (see p188).

★ Royal Yacht Britannia

T 555 5566 , www.royalyachtbritannia.co.uk *Oct-Mar daily 1000-1530; Apr-Sep daily 0930-1630. Closes 1½ hrs after last admission. Adults £8, concessions £6, children £4, family (2 adults, 3 children) £20. Brittania Tour bus from Waverley Bridge (see p27) or buses 11, 22, 34, 35 and 36 from Princes St.* Map 6, A6, p256

The Britannia is a genuinely fascinating attraction and shows the Windsors in a strangely downbeat manner. The relatively steep entrance fee may seem excessive, but it's well worth it. The introductory video is mawkish but at least brings home the yacht's significant role in post-war British history. Then there's a brief display of various bits and pieces from the old girl (the ship, not Liz) and it's on to the main course. Staunch republicans will grudgingly applaud the restraint while ardent monarchists may be horrified at the astonishingly ordinary scale of things.

The tour of the yacht is conducted by audio handset which gives you 55 minutes of everything you ever wanted to know about the royals at sea (minus the juicy details). This is no floating palace – more a working ship very much designed and furnished to a strict budget. Remember that the ship was fitted out in the 1950s at a time when even the royal family must have been aware of the prevailing atmosphere of austerity. Still, this is a vessel which was in use until 1997, and the sight of Her Majesty's bedroom, more in keeping with a mid-range guest-house than a Head of State's private quarters, comes as a real shock. Another shock is the sight of kitchen staff going about their business, a reminder that the yacht is frequently booked for corporate dinners and the like. Overall, the whole effect is a bizarre mix of scout camp, Carry On and early James Bond – in other words it's like being in a late-50s time warp, and strangely soothing. The public rooms are a bit more ostentatious, especially the dining room, but considering the impressive roll call of names who have been entertained here – including Nelson Mandela, the Clintons and the honeymooning Charles and Diana – this can be forgiven. The drawing room, on the other hand, shows the Queen's penchant for chintz and would be more at home in rural Berkshire. The tour offers a genuine insight into the lives of the royal family and it's no surprise that some of them were less than happy at the prospect of the yacht being accessible to the likes of you and me.

! A young Sean Connery worked at Portobello pool as a life-guard before he made it big – yesh.

Newhaven

A 10-min walk from the Royal Yacht Britannia, or take buses 7, 10, 11 or 16 from the top of Leith Walk. Map 6, p256

Newhaven was once a busy fishing community and one of the most colourful parts of Edinburgh. The fishing industry has all but disappeared and, though the little fishermen's cottages have been restored, there is no life left in the place, other than the occasional pleasure yacht in the harbour. The village's maritime past is told in the **Newhaven Heritage Museum** (*daily 1200-1700, free*), which occupies part of the old fishmarket overlooking the harbour.

Portobello

Buses 15, 26, 42, 66, X86 from Princes St.

About five miles east of the city centre is the Georgian seaside resort of Portobello, which originated in the mid-18th century when a retired sailor, George Hamilton, built a cottage here named Puerta Bella. It soon became a popular seaside resort with Edinburgh's upper classes, due to the lack of public transport from the city, thus restricting access for the hoi polloi. The long, sandy beach is still quite busy on sunny days, and there are the usual amusement arcades, funfairs, chips and ice cream.

Museums and galleries

- **City Arts Centre** Large municipal gellery featuring native artists and temporary exhibitions, p44.
- **Collective Gallery** Leading space for seeing the work of emerging Scottish-based artists, p44.
- **Dean Gallery** Comprehensive collections of Dadaist and Surrealist art, p90.
- **Dynamic Earth** Multi-media exhibition telling the story of our planet – both educational and entertaining, p53.
- **Edinburgh Printmakers Workshop and Gallery** 23 Union St, off Leith Walk, **T** 557 2479. *Tue-Sat 1000-1800. Free.* Huge range of contemporary etchings, lithographs and screenprints.
- **Edinburgh University Collection of Historic Musical Instruments** Does what it says on the tin, p66.
- **Fruitmarket Gallery** Small space for cutting edge works, p44.
- **John Knox House** Nice house, shame about the austere displays inside, p46.
- **Leith Gallery** 65 The Shore, **T** 553 5255, www.the-leith-gallery.co.uk Leading gallery in Scottish contemporary art.
- **Museum of Childhood** Lots of toys, games, hyperactive kiddies and nostalgic adults, p46.
- **Museum of Edinburgh** Uneven display of the city's history housed in the 16th century Huntly House, p48.
- **Museum of Pathology and Anatomy** Working museum for the study of human disease, p62.
- **National Gallery of Scotland** Houses the most important collection of old masters in the UK outside London, p72.

Museums and galleries

- **Newhaven Heritage Museum** Tiny museum that tells the story of this erstwhile fishing village, p102.
- **Open Eye Gallery** 75-79 Cumberland St, **T** 557 1020. *Mon-Fri 1000-1800, Sat 1000-1600*. Hosts a fast-changing round of selling shows of work by artists in Scotland.
- **People's Story Museum** Focuses on the real heroes of history – the common people, p48.
- **Royal Scottish Academy** Used to stage major temporary exhibitions, re-opens in August 2003 after extensive refurbishment, p72.
- **Scottish National Gallery of Modern Art** Strong on the main players of Expressionism and 20th century Scottish painters, p88
- **Scottish National Portrait Gallery** Part art gallery, part Scottish history lesson, it also houses the National Collection of Photography, p77.
- **Shaping a Nation** Not altogether serious look at Scotland's role in the world and famous Scots, p93.
- **Sir Jules Thorn Exhibition of the History of Surgery and Dental Museum** Fairly grotesque but fun look through the keyhole of surgical history, p64.
- **Stills Gallery** Changing photographic exhibitions, p44
- **Talbot Rice Gallery** The University's collection of European Renaissance painting, housed in a wonderful neoclassical building, p62
- **Writer's Museum** Homage to the lives and works of Burns, Stevenson and Scott , p39.
- *For a full list of smaller private art galleries and details of forthcoming exhibitions pick up a copy of the latest monthly issue of the Edinburgh Gallery Guide, or visit www.edinburgh-galleries.co.uk*

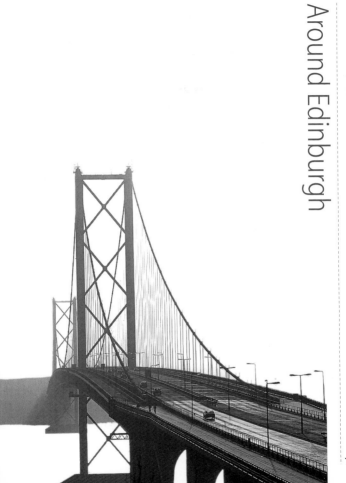

West of the city 107 The Forth Rail Bridge is one of the great engineering feats of the 19th century, while the aristoctratic splendour of Hopetoun House and elegantly wasted royal palace at Linlithgow, in the region of West Lothian, are both highlights – no question.

South of the city 110 Hill-walkers can take advantage of the wide open spaces of the Pentland Hills, and the esoteric secrets of Rosslyn Chapel will beguile everyone from keen historians to New Age theorists.

East of the city 112 Miles of great golf courses, ruined cliff-top castles and soft, sandy beaches characterize the East Lothian coast but the real feather in the cap is the Bass Rock, a lump of basalt lying just offshore. This giant lop-sided loaf, home to huge seabird colonies, is enough to steam up the binocular lenses of even the most guano-hardened birdwatcher.

West of the city

*Though Edinburgh is the least claustrophobic of cities, there are those who will wish to take advantage of the many interesting and beautiful places to visit outside its boundaries. It's worth taking a train across the magnificent **Forth Rail Bridge** to North Queensferry, for instance, or one of the many river cruises to see it from below. Further west are two of the country's most appealing historical sights, **Hopetoun House** and **Linlithgow Palace**.*

▸▸ *See Eating and drinking p167, Tours p26*

Sights

South Queensferry
First Edinburgh buses 43 and 47 from St Andrews bus station (20 mins).

Ten miles west of Edinburgh is the ancient town of South Queensferry. The town's narrow main street is lined with lovely old buildings, most striking of which is the row of two-tiered shops. The small **museum** on the High Street *(Mon, Thu, Fri and Sat 1000-1300 and 1415-1700, free)* traces the town's history and the building of the road and rail bridges while the **Hawes Inn**, in the shadow of the rail bridge, featured in RL Stevenson's *Kidnapped*.

The town is dominated by the two great bridges that tower overhead on either side, spanning the Firth of Forth at its narrowest point. The massive steel cantilevered **Forth Rail Bridge**, over 1½ miles long and 360 ft high, is a staggering monument to Victorian engineering. It was built in 1883-90 and 60,000 tons of steel were used in its construction. Beside it is the **Forth Road Bridge**, a suspension bridge built between 1958 and 1964, which ended the 900 year-old ferry crossing between South and North Queensferry. The Road Bridge is open to pedestrians, and it's worth walking across for the views of the Rail Bridge.

Dalmeny House

T 331 1888, www.dalmeny.co.uk *Bus from St Andrew bus station to Chapel Gate, 1 mile from the house, or you can take a train (20 mins) which stops at the village station. Sun-Tue 1400-1730 in Jul and Aug only. Adults £4, concessions £3, children £2.*

Less than a mile from South Queensferry is Dalmeny House, the Earl of Rosebery's home for over 300 years. The present house, built in 1815 in Tudor Gothic, contains a superb collection of 18th-century French furniture, porcelain and tapestries and paintings, including portraits by Gainsborough, Raeburn, Reynolds and Lawrence. There is also a fascinating collection of Napoleon Bonaparte memorabilia, assembled by the fifth Earl of Rosebery, a former Prime Minister. The house can also be reached from the other side of the River Almond at Cramond (see p95); it's a two-mile walk.

★ Hopetoun House

T 331 2451, www.hopetounhouse.com *Daily Apr-Oct 1000-1730. Adults £6, concessions £5, children £3.*

Two miles west of South Queensferry is Hopetoun House, which thoroughly deserves its reputation as "Scotland's finest stately home". Set in 100 acres of magnificent parkland, including the Red Deer park, the house is the epitome of aristocratic grandeur, and recently celebrated its 300th birthday. Hopetoun House is perhaps the finest example of the work of William Burn and William Adam. It was built for the Earls of Hopetoun, later created Marquesses of Linlithgow, and part of the house is still lived in by the current Marquess of Linlithgow and his family. The house contains a large collection of art treasures and the grounds are also open to the public. You could come here and pretend you're a member of the aristocracy for the day, then go back to your humble B&B and weep.

North Queensferry
Frequent trains from Waverley and Haymarket (30 mins).

Cowering beneath the massive structure of the Forth Rail Bridge, North Queensferry provides the ideal vantage point from which to wonder at this fantastic 19th-century engineering feat. Also here is the popular **Deep Sea World**, Scotland's award-winning national aquarium, see Kids, p223.

Inchcolm Island
The island can only be reached as part of a cruise. See Tours, p26.

In the Firth of Forth sits the tiny island of Inchcolm. Known as the Iona of the East, the island's famous **Abbey of St Columba** was founded in 1123 for Augustinian monks by King Alexander I. Although sacked many times by the English and desecrated during the Reformation, the abbey is remarkably well preserved and includes one of Scotland's rare 13th-century octagonal chapter houses and 14th-century cloisters. These are the finest monastic buildings left in the country. You can also climb the tower for great views of the island, which is populated by nesting seabirds and a colony of seals.

★ Linlithgow Palace
T 01506-842896, www.historic-scotland.gov.uk *Apr-Sep daily 0930-1830; Oct-Mar Mon-Sat 0930-1630, Sun 1400-1630. Adults £3, concessions £2.30, children £1. Hourly trains to and from Edinburgh (20 mins) and regular buses from St Andrew bus station.*

The pleasant little West Lothian town of Linlithgow is where you'll find the Renaissance Linlithgow Palace, one of the most romantic and impressive historic buildings in Scotland. It's off the beaten track and relatively little-visited but well worth the detour. The 15th-century ruin is set on the edge of Linlithgow

Loch and is associated with many of Scotland's main historical players, including James V (1512) and Mary, Queen of Scots (1542), who were both born here. James V was also married here, to Mary of Guise, and Bonnie Prince Charlie popped in for a visit during the 1745 rebellion. One year later the palace was badly damaged by fire during its occupation by General Hawley's troops, prior to their defeat by Jacobite forces under Prince Charles at the Battle of Falkirk. The ruin still conveys a real sense of the sheer scale of the lavish lifestyle of the court, from the ornate fountain in the inner courtyard to the magnificent Great Hall with its massive kitchens. Next to the palace is St Michael's Church, the larges pre-Reformation church in the country, with its controversial crown and spire, added in 1964.

South of the city

*Immediately south of Edinburgh, across the city bypass, are the wild and rugged **Pentland Hills**, great for a bracing Sunday walk, and the magical, mystical **Rosslyn Chapel**, with its cache of weird and wonderful secrets.*

 Sights

Pentland Hills
OS Landranger Map No 66 covers the area.

South of the Braid Hills, beyond the City Bypass, are Edinburgh's Pentland Hills, a range of serious hills, remote in parts, rising to almost 2,000 ft and which stretch some 16 miles from the outskirts of Edinburgh to Lanarkshire. The hills offer relatively painless climbs and you'll be rewarded with magnificent views once you reach the top. On the northern slopes of the Pentlands is the village of Swanston, a huddle of 18th-century thatched, white-washed cottages. The largest of these, Swanston Cottage, was the holiday home of the Stevenson family, where the sickly young Robert Louis spent his summers. There are many paths up to the various Pentland summits and round the lochs and reservoirs. The main access is the A702, which passes the Midlothian Ski Centre at Hillend (see Sports, p213). There's a marked walking trail up to the ski slope, or you can take the chair lift. At the top of the slope it's a short walk to Caerketton Hill for fantastic panoramic views of Edinburgh, the Firth of Forth and the hills of Fife and Stirlingshire.

★ Rosslyn Chapel

T 440 2159, www.rosslynchapel.org.uk Mon-Sat 1000-1700, Sun 1200-1645. Adults £4, concessions £3.50, children £1. Bus 315 from Princes St to Roslin every ¼-1 hr (40 mins), or take bus 37 from Charlotte Sq to Loanhead and change to the 141 to Roslin (£3.20 return). A taxi takes around 20 mins and costs £15.

Seven miles south of Edinburgh, just off the A701 to Penicuik, lies the little village of Roslin (yes, it is spelled differently), home of the 15th-century Rosslyn Chapel. Perched above the North Esk, the magnificent chapel has a richly carved interior full of Biblical representations and pagan and masonic symbols, and has been described as "a fevered hallucination in stone". Foundations were laid in 1446 for a much larger church which was never built. What exists is the Lady Chapel, inspiration of Sir William Sinclair, who himself supervised masons brought from abroad who took 40 years to complete it to his design. According to legend, his grandfather, the adventurer Prince Henry of Orkney, set foot in the New World a century before Columbus. This is backed up by the carvings of various New World plants. One of the most fascinating sights in the church, and the most elaborate carving, is the Prentice Pillar. Legend has it that while the master mason was away in Rome making additional drawings to complete the pillar, an apprentice finished it for him. On the mason's return he murdered the apprentice in a fury. Speculation as to the purpose of the chapel dwells on esoteric secrets, and a plethora of recent books claim that the Holy Grail, supposedly brought from the East by the Knights Templar, is buried here. Whether or not you believe this, you'll still find its architecture and atmosphere fascinating. Once you've seen the chapel, there are some very pleasant walks in near-by Roslin Glen, from where you get great views of Roslin Castle.

East of the city

East Lothian *stretches east from Musselburgh, to the east of Edinburgh, along the coast to North Berwick and Dunbar. This is real golfing country, with a string of excellent courses running the length of the coast, and there are miles of sandy beaches. The East Lothian coast is also home to huge colonies of seabirds, especially on the* **Bass Rock***, a dramatic volcanic islet off* **North Berwick***. Inland is the attractive historic market town of* **Haddington** *and the excellent* **Museum of Flight***. There are good transport links with Edinburgh – trains stop in Musselburgh and North Berwick, and there are regular buses to all the main towns.*

▸▸ *See Eating and drinking p168, Sports p211*

 ## Sights

Musselburgh
Trains from Waverley station North Berwick stop in Musselburgh.

Six miles east of Edinburgh, across the River Esk, is the town of Musselburgh. It's a fairly humdrum place, but may be of interest to golfing enthusiasts as the original home of golf. It is also a target for naturalists who come to see the huge populations of migrating waders, ducks and seabirds. Ice cream lovers may also be interested to note that *Luca's* on the High Street has most of the competition licked (see also p224).

Aberlady

Buses from St Andrew station to North Berwick stop in Aberlady.

Further east is the conservation village of Aberlady, at the mouth of the River Peffer. A row of Georgian cottages lines the main street and there's a lovely old church which hints at Aberlady's erstwhile importance as a port. The old harbour is silted up and now forms part of the mudflats and salt marshes of the Aberlady Bay Nature Reserve, home to numerous seabirds.

Gullane

Buses from St Andrew station to North Berwick stop in Gullane.

Gullane is a resort town with an exclusive air which is hopelessly devoted to golf. There are no fewer than four golf courses surrounding Gullane, including Muirfield with its antediluvian attitudes. Windsurfing has recently been gaining in popularity, offering a more democratic alternative.

Dirleton Castle

T 01620-850330, www.historic-scotland.gov.uk *Apr-Sep daily 0930-1830; Oct-Mar Mon-Sat 0930-1630, Sun 1400-1630. Adults £3, concessions £2.30, children £1.*

Between Gullane and North Berwick is the attractive little village of Dirleton, dominated by its ruined castle which dates from the 12th century. The gorgeous gardens, which date from the 16th century, are well worth a visit. At the eastern end of the village a road runs north for a mile or so to Yellowcraigs, where there's a lovely clean beach and views across to Fidra Island.

North Berwick

Scottish Seabird Centre, **T** 01620-890202, www.seabird.org *Daily 1000-1800 in summer; 1000-1600 in winter. Adults £4.95, children and concessions £3.35. £7.50 including rail travel from Scotrail, see p23). There are frequent buses (124, X5) and trains from Edinburgh.*

The dignified and slightly faded Victorian seaside resort of North Berwick lies half and hour east of Edinburgh. The main attraction is the excellent **Scottish Sea Bird Centre** by the harbour. It has live footage of puffins and gannets nesting on nearby Fidra and Bass Rock. There are also various displays and interactive technology. The town also has some good sandy **beaches** and two excellent **golf courses**, the West Links and the Glen. North Berwick is overlooked by **Berwick Law**, a 613-ft volcanic crag. It's an easy walk to the top, and the views on a clear day are rewarding. Take Law Road out of town and then follow the signs.

Bass Rock and Fidra

www.north-berwick.co.uk/bass

Three miles offshore is the 350 ft-high Bass Rock, a massive, guano-covered lump of basalt, used as a prison in the 17th century but now home to millions of nesting gannets and other seabirds including guillemots, razorbills and fulmars. There are also puffins nesting on the nearby island of Fidra. Sir David Attenborough described the Bass Rock as one of the 12 wildlife wonders of the world, so obviously it is well worth taking a closer look. There are boat trips (about 1¼ hours) from North Berwick, weather permitting, to the Bass Rock and Fidra, daily between May and September with Chris Marr, **T** 01620-892838, sula2@bosinternet.com

★ Tantallon Castle

T 01620-892727, www.historic-scotland.gov.uk *Apr-Sep daily 0930-1830; Oct-Mar Mon-Wed and Sat 0930-1630, Thu 0930-1200, Fri and Sun 1400-1630. Adults £3, concessions £2.30, children £1. Take the Dunbar bus from North Berwick (see p114).*

Three miles east of North Berwick, off the A198, are the mid-14th-century ruins of Tantallon Castle, perched on the edge of the cliffs, looking out to the Bass Rock. This formidable fortress was the strong-hold of the 'Red Douglases', Earls of Angus, until Cromwell's attack in 1651, which left only the 50 ft-high curtain wall intact.

● *There's a great beach a few miles south of Tantallon. Turn left off the A198 at Auldhame Farm, follow the road for about a mile to the gate (small toll charge) and beyond to the car park.*

Haddington and around

First Edinburgh run regular buses to and from St Andrew bus station. There are also hourly buses to North Berwick (Mon-Sat, less frequently on Sun; 45 mins).

Handsome Haddington is a prosperous country town only 15 miles east of Edinburgh, making it ideal for a pleasant day out from the rigours of city life. The compact town centre is a very attractive place to stroll around. No fewer than 129 buildings have been listed as historically interesting, including the graceful **Town House**, in tree-lined Court Street, which was built in 1748 by William Adam, father of Robert. At the east end of the High Street, Church Street leads to **St Mary's Collegiate Church**, the largest parish church in Scotland, dating from the 14th century and restored in the 1970s. It's a particularly beautiful ecclesiastical building and enjoys a lovely setting on the river (*Apr-Sep Mon-Sat 1100-1600, Sun 1400-1630, free*). Buried in the churchyard is Jane Welsh (1801-66), wife of essayist and historian Thomas Carlyle. The **Jane Welsh Carlyle Museum**, at 2 Lodge Street, was her home until her marriage, and part of it is open to the public (*Apr-Sep Wed-Sat 1400-1700, adults, £1.50, concessions £1*).

One mile south of Haddington is **Lennoxlove House**, seat of the Duke of Hamilton. Inside are some fine paintings and furniture, but the pièce de resistance is the death mask of Mary, Queen of Scots, and a silver casket in which she kept her letters, given to her by her first husband, Francis II of France (*Easter-Oct Wed, Thu, Sun and some Sats 1400-1630, adults £4, children £2*).

★ Museum of Flight

East Fortune Airfield, **T** 01620-880308. *Easter-Oct daily 1030-1700 (Jul-Aug till 1800); Nov-Easter daily 1030-1600. Easter-Oct: adults £3, concessions £1.50, children free. Nov-Easter: adults £1.50, concessions £0.75. Bus 121 from North Berwick or Haddington several times daily Apr-Sep.*

Four miles northeast of Haddington, at East Fortune, is the Museum of Flight, Scotland's National Museum of Aviation. Housed in a complex of Second World War hangars and nissen huts, it's a vast and impressive collection of old aircraft and wartime memorabilia.

Edinburgh has a huge selection of places to stay, more than any other city in Britain outside London. At the top end of the scale, there are some fabulously luxurious hotels which offer a chance to enjoy a taste of aristocratic grandeur and style. Most of these are in the New Town, West End and around Calton Hill. Many city centre hotels offer good deals during the low season, especially at weekends, and also offer a standby room rate throughout the year. There are also hundreds of guesthouses and B&Bs, mostly concentrated in the southern suburbs of Bruntsfield and Newington, Pilrig to the northeast of the city centre heading towards Leith, and along Corstorphine Road to the west. At the lower end of the scale there are several hostels, most of which are central, and a couple of campsites which are not too far from the centre. Most of the universities and colleges offer campus accommodation, but this is neither cheap nor centrally located. Another option, if you're staying a week or more, are serviced apartments, which can be cost-effective and also come with their own security and parking.

£ **Sleeping codes**

L	over £160	D	£50-70
A	£130-160	E	£30-50
B	£90-130	F	under £30
C	£70-90		

Prices are based on the cost of a double room in high season, or, in the case of hostels, for a bed in a dormitory or shared room.

If you arrive in Edinburgh without a reservation, particularly during the Festival or at Hogmanay, the chances are you won't find a room anywhere near the centre. It pays to book well in advance. The tourist office (see p30) sends out its accommodation brochure for free so that you can book a place yourself, or their Central Reservations Service, **T** 473 3855, centres@eltb.org, will make a reservation for you, for a non-refundable fee of £5.

For those spending several days in the city there's the alternative option of renting a serviced or self-catering apartment. Prices range from around £200 per week right up to £800 and above, depending on the type of accommodation, and there's usually a minimum stay of anything from two nights up to one week. Several serviced apartments in the city are listed in this guide. A good source of self-catering accommodation is the Scottish Tourist Board guide (£5.95), which is available from any tourist office. There are several independent hostels in the city which are less rigorous than the SYHA ones and are open 24 hours. It's best to arrive around 1100-1130 if you don't have a booking, but even outside the high season it's not always easy to find a bed in the city centre. Edinburgh's universities open their halls of residence to visitors during the summer vacation (late June to September), and some also during the Easter and Christmas breaks. Contact the British Universities Accommodation Consortium for a brochure; **T** 0115-9504571.

Note that single rooms are in short supply and many places are reluctant to let a double room to one person, even when they're not busy. Single rooms are usually more than the cost per person for a double room, and in some cases cost the same as two people sharing a double room .

Old Town

Hotels, guesthouses and B&Bs

L Apex International Hotel, 31-35 Grassmarket, **T** 300 3456, **F** 220 5345, www.apexhotels.co.uk *Map 2, H2, p248* 175 en suite rooms. Large, recently converted former University building in the heart of the Old Town. Top floor rooms with Castle views are more expensive but worth the extra. *Metro* bar-restaurant on the ground floor is good for a drink. Recently opened, but not visited at the time of writing is the Apex City Hotel, 61 Grassmarket, **T** 243 3456, which is aiming to be more upmarket and therefore more expensive.

L Crowne Plaza Hotel, 80 High St, **T** 557 9797, **F** 557 9789, www.crowneplazaed.co.uk *Map 2, E6, p248* 238 en suite rooms, three with disabled facilities. Slap bang in the heart of it all, half-way between the Castle and Holyrood Palace, this monster of a hotel has been sympathetically designed to blend in with the surr-ounding architecture. Plush and with most of the trimmings you'd expect at this price, but perhaps a bit impersonal. Very popular location, with parking, fitness suite and pool, restaurant and bar.

L Scotsman Hotel, North Bridge, **T** 556 5565, www.scotsman hotel.co.uk *Map 2, D6, p248* 68 rooms and suites. The former offices of *The Scotsman* newspaper have been transformed into this state-of-the-art boutique hotel. Each room is distinctive and has been furnished with great attention to detail, with original art,

DVD and internet and its very own Edinburgh Monopoly board. Services and facilities include valet parking, screening room, bar, brasserie and restaurant, breakfast room, private dining rooms and a Health Club and Spa with a stainless steel pool (see p211). This represents the highest standards of style and luxury the city has to offer, but it comes at a price, especially the Penthouse Suite which will set you back nearly a grand for the night. Off-peak rates are available from as little as £70 per person.

L The Witchery by the Castle, Castlehill, Royal Mile, **T** 225 0973, **F** 220 4392, www.thewitchery.com *Map 2, F2, p248* Upstairs from the acclaimed restaurant (see p143) are six suites which really have to be seen to be believed. Regularly featured in all the posh travel mags as the most romantic place to stay, Cosmo even went as far as to describe The Witchery as one of 'seven wonders'. Each suite is a vision of Gothic theatrical excess, with velvet drapes, four-poster beds, 18th-century oak paneling, marble bathrooms and more antiques and historic portraits than you'd find in the average museum. Additional touches include a complimentary bottle of champers, home-made cookies, DVD and CD library. Four new suites have recently been opened across the road in 17th-century Sempill's Court. Accommodation in Scotland's capital just doesn't get any sexier than this, so make sure he or she is worth it.

B Bank Hotel, 1 South Bridge, **T** 556 9043, **F** 558 1362, www.festival-inns.co.uk *Map 2, E6, p248* Nine individually themed rooms, each based on a famous Scot, from the poetry of Robert Burns to the designs of Charles Rennie Mackintosh, and all tastefully done. Well-situated in the haggis belt. Hotel reception is in Logie Baird's bar at street level and this is also where breakfast is served. A good deal for this part of town.

B Jurys Inn, 43 Jeffrey St, **T** 200 3300, **F** 200 0400, bookings@ jurysdoyle.com *Map 2, E7, p249* 186 en suite rooms. Huge

Best

Hip hotels

- Scotsman Hotel, p120
- Malmaison Hotel, p138
- Point Hotel, p133
- Ricks, p126

converted office block. Functional but comfortable and an unbeatable location close to the Royal Mile, Princes Street and Waverley Station. Some rooms have been adapted for disabled visitors. On-street parking. Cheaper during the week (Sunday-Thursday) when the stags and hens have departed.

B Tailors Hall Hotel, 139 Cowgate, **T** 622 6801, **F** 622 6818, tailors@festival-inns.co.uk *Map 2, G5, p248* 42 en suite rooms. Above the busy *Three Sisters* pub, so quiet hideaway this ain't. Aimed at the late and loud crowd who take advantage of the disco downstairs and the courtyard seating. Don't expect much sleep during the Festival. Even better value if three or four share a room.

C Hotel Ibis, 6 Hunter Sq, **T** 240 7000, **F** 240 7007. *Map 2, F6, p248* 99 en suite rooms. Part of the Accor group, this modern hotel is handy for everything but doesn't exactly blend in with its historic surroundings. Continental breakfast £4.95 extra. Low season discounts. Characterless but very good value.

D Premier Lodge, 94-96 Grassmarket, **T** 0870 700 1370, **F** 0870 700 1371, www.premierlodge.com *Map 2, G3, p248* 44 en suite rooms. Basic and close to the action. Ideal for those on a budget who like to stay out late.

D-E Travelodge, 33 St Mary's St, **T** 557 6281, **F** 557 3681, www.travelodge.co.uk *Map 2, F8, p249* Nothing fancy, just a good-sized clean and comfortable room, but great location and good value. Parking. Breakfast £7.95 extra.

Serviced apartments

L-A Holyrood Aparthotel, 1 Nether Bakehouse, Holyrood, **T** 524 3200, **F** 524 3210, www.holyroodaparthotel.com *Map 2, E9, p249* 41 luxury two-bedroom apartments, fully-equipped and with a high-tech, contemporary look. Facilities include gym and underground parking. Cheaper for three or four sharing. Well situated, close to the new Parliament and Royal Mile.

Hostels

E St Christopher's Inns, 9-13 Market St, **T** 226 1446, **F** 226 1447, www.st-christophers.co.uk *Map 2, E5, p248* Part of a select European chain, perfectly placed for Waverley Station, Princes Street and the Old Town. Accommodation ranges from 4-10 bed dorms with shower in each, to singles (£40) and twins. Includes continental breakfast.

E-F Central Youth Hostel, 4 Robertson Close, Cowgate. *Map 2, G5, p248* SYHA hostel which is only open during July and August. For bookings, contact the Eglinton SYHA (see p134).

E-F Edinburgh Backpackers Hostel, 65 Cockburn St, **T** 220 1717, **F** 539 8695, info@ hoppo.com *Map 2, E6, p248* 97 beds in 10 dormitories, four doubles and one triple. Just off the Royal Mile, so busy and noisy. More expensive in private rooms. No curfew.

E-F Brodie's Backpacker Hostel, 12 High St, **T/F** 556 6770, www.brodieshostels.co.uk *Map 2, E7, p249* Smaller and cosier than the other city centre hostels, with only four dorms. Friendly and good range of facilities.

F Castle Rock Hostel, 15 Johnston Terr, **T** 225 9666, **F** 226 5078, castle-rock@ scotlands-top-hostels.com *Map 2, G2, p248* Prime location below the Castle. Vast building with 250 beds in 20 dorms. No singles or doubles.

F High Street Hostel, 8 Blackfriars St, **T** 557 3984, high-street@ scotlands-top-hostels.com *Map 2, F7, p249* Long-established backpacker hang-out. 16 dorms. Cheap, lively and right in the thick of the action, between the sights of the Royal Mile and nightlife of the Cowgate. They also run their own (free) Old Town tour.

F Royal Mile Backpackers, 105 High St, **T** 557 6120, royalmile@ scotlands-top-hostels.com *Map 2, E7, p249* Small, cosy hostel with 38 beds in five dorms. Lively and great value. Same group as the Castle Rock and High Street hostels (see above). All open 24 hours and offer an optional breakfast for £1.90.

New Town

Hotels, guesthouses and B&Bs

L Albany Hotel, 39-43 Albany St, **T** 556 0397, **F** 557 6633, 1237@compuserve.com *Map 3, G8, p251* 21 rooms. New Town Georgian elegance and bourgeois charm only a few minutes from Princes Street. High degree of intimacy created by the rich furnishings and discreet attention. Excellent basement restaurant, *Haldane's*, see p157.

L Balmoral Hotel, 1 Princes St, **T** 556 2414, **F** 557 3747, www.roccofortehotels.com/balmoral *Map 2, C5, p248* 188 en suite rooms. Century-old Edinburgh landmark above Waverley station. From the modern and luxurious entrance hall to the magnificent city views in the upper rooms, the Balmoral oozes class. The Presidential suite has housed the rich and (in)famous, from Mick Jagger to Henry Kissinger. Its main restaurant, Number One, is excellent and the brasserie, Hadrian's, less grand but good value (see p154). Those who can't afford it can at least get a taster by taking afternoon tea in the soft leather booths of the Palm Court to the accompaniment of a chamber orchestra.

L **George Intercontinental**, 19-21 George St, **T** 225 1251 **F** 226 5644, www.edinburgh. intercontinental.com *Map 2, C2, p248* 195 en suite rooms. Grand Adam building conveniently located on Edinburgh's smartest street and very popular with international visitors, especially during the Festival. Rooms are well-equipped and some have office facilities. Good restaurant.

L **The Howard**, 34 Great King St, **T** 557 3500, **F** 557 6515, www.thehoward.com *Map 3, F6, p250* 18 en suite rooms. Beautiful Georgian townhouse, the epitome of quiet, understated New Town elegance and famous for its chintzy luxury. Such privilege doesn't come cheap, however, and The Howard is more expensive than most. Its basement restaurant, *36*, serves the very best of modern Scottish cuisine in contemporary, minimalist surroundings.

L **Roxburghe Hotel**, 38 Charlotte Sq, **T** 240 5500, **F** 240 5555, info@roxburghe.macdonald-hotels.co.uk *Map 4, A10, p253* 197 en suite rooms. Lovely Georgian building in Edinburgh's financial heart and on its loveliest square. This classic Adam building has undergone a recent facelift and is now as stunning inside as out. Restaurant and less formal bistro.

A **Christopher North House Hotel**, 6 Gloucester Pl, **T** 225 2720, **F** 220 4706, www.christophernorth.co.uk *Map 3, G5, p250* 14 en suite rooms. Elegant Georgian building with stylish contemporary décor inside. Rates include full Scottish breakfast. Leisure and conference facilities.

B Ricks, 55a Frederick St, **T** 622 7800, **F** 622 7801, www.ricks edinburgh.co.uk *Map 4, A12, p253* Not so much a hotel as a restaurant with rooms. The 10 very sleek and stylish rooms are accessed via a staircase at the rear of the bar-restaurant, but soundproofing means that late-night revellers don't keep you awake. Decor is subtle, furnishings unfussy and in-room entertainment includes CD and DVD players and minibar. Night-owls have the huge advantage of being able to take breakfast (not included in price) in the downstairs restaurant, thereby avoiding an uncivilized wake-up call. Of all the new boutique hotels around town, this is the grooviest. Book well ahead during the Festival and Hogmanay.

B Royal Scots Club, 30 Abercromby Pl, **T** 556 4270, **F** 558 3769, www.scotsclub.co.uk *Map 2, A2, p248* 22 en suite rooms. Small, cosy and traditional hotel housed in a classic Georgian townhouse. There's a real gentleman's club atmosphere and the rooms are tastefully furnished, some with four-poster beds and views of the Firth of Forth.

B 17 Abercromby Place, 17 Abercromby Pl, **T** 557 8036, **F** 558 3453. *Map 2, A2, p248* Nine rooms. Classic townhouse hotel and former home of renowned New Town architect, William Playfair. Sumptuous style and superb views.

C 24 Northumberland Place, 24 Northumberland Pl, **T** 556 8140, **F** 556 4423 www.ingrams.co.uk *Map 3, G6, p250* Run by David and Theresa Ingram, very friendly, welcoming and engaging hosts who offer a quality of service lacking in most B&Bs. Three en suite rooms, all very comfortable and tastefully decorated, as you'd expect from a former antique dealer. Crucially, there's parking at the rear, a rare commodity in the New Town. No sign outside so very discreet. Booking ahead essential.

Serviced apartments

L-A Royal Garden Apartments, York Buildings, Queen St, **T** 625 1234, www.royalgarden.co.uk *Map 2, A3, p248* Opposite the Scottish National Portrait Gallery and handy for Broughton village and George Street. Sumptuously furnished self-catering apartments with bags of space, satellite TV, a CD player, designer fitted kitchen and views across the Firth of Forth, and access to Queen Street Gardens. Limited parking. Café serving breakfast and snacks. Apartments cost from £150 for a one-bedroom apartment to £325 for a penthouse sleeping up to six. Great for families.

Hostels

F Princes Street Backpackers, 5 West Register St, **T** 556 6984, www.princesstbackpackers.com *Map 2, C4, p248* At the east end of Princes Street and near the bus station. 120 beds. Cheap, basic and very popular. Great value breakfast and free Sunday dinner.

Calton Hill and Broughton

Hotels, guesthouses and B&Bs

L The Glasshouse, 2 Greenside Pl, T0777-6003890, www.theetongroup.com *Map 2, A6, p248* 65 rooms. This new luxury boutique hotel, which opened in May 2003, is on the top floor of the Omni leisure complex and is entered via the original façade of a Victorian church. Most rooms have their own balconies and great views. Features a two-acre roof garden with superb views and a rooftop bar. The rooms are stylish and contemporary, complementing the sleek glass exterior.

L Parliament House Hotel, 15 Calton Hill, **T** 478 4000, **F** 478 4001, www.scotland-hotels.co.uk *Map 2, B6, p248* 54 rooms. Smart, centrally located townhouse close to east end of Princes Street. Ask for a room with a view. Continental breakfast only. Has rooms for disabled visitors.

L Royal Terrace Hotel, 18 Royal Terr, **T** 557 3222, **F** 557 5334. *Map 3, G11, p251* 108 rooms. Exquisitely furnished rooms, most with whirlpool spa and, though it may be a bit OTT for some tastes, there's no denying this is the height of decadent over-indulgence. Sports facilities include pool, sauna and gym, and there's a lovely terraced garden at the rear. Bar and restaurant.

A Mansfield House, 57 Dublin St, **T** 556 7980, www.mansfield guesthouse.com *Map 3, G8, p251* Top of the range exclusively gay guesthouse. Each of the nine bedrooms is designed individually, in styles ranging from black and white, to gothic to camp, to ultra luxury. Cheaper without en suite. Continental breakfast included.

B Stuart House, 12 East Claremont St, **T** 557 9030, **F** 557 0563, www.stuartguesthouse.co.uk *Map 3, F8, p251* Five en suite rooms. Comfortable and well-furnished rooms in Georgian-style townhouse. A short walk from Broughton Street and New Town.

C Greenside Hotel, 9 Royal Terr, **T/F** 557 0022, www.townhouse hotels.co.uk *Map 3, G11, p251* 16 en suite rooms. Close to Princes Street and Waverley Station. Elegant Georgian house with well-appointed rooms and a nice garden at the back. Dinner available by arrangement. Good value at this price.

B Alva House, 45 Alva Pl, **T** 558 1382. www.alvahouse.com *Map 1, p247* Five rooms, one ensuite. Men-only guesthouse in the Abbeyhill colonies, just off the London Road, with continental breakfast from 0800-1200.

B Garlands Guest House, 48 Pilrig St, **T** 554 4205, www.garlands.demon.co.uk *Map 3, D11, p251* Six en suite rooms. Bill and Ian have been running this gay friendly Georgian B&B for the last seven years.

C Ardmor House, 74 Pilrig St, **T** 554 4944, www.ardmorhouse.com *Map 3, C11, p251* Five rooms. Stylish Victorian townhouse which combines original features with contemporary design. Gay-owned, straight friendly. Owners also have **Ardmor Apartment**, at 3/1 Gayfield Street. This luxury self-catering apartment, in a quiet street opposite CC Blooms bar and nightclub, sleeps up to four with a minimum stay of four nights.

Stockbridge and Inverleith

Hotels, guesthouses and B&Bs

L Channings, 12-16 South Learmonth Gdns, **T** 315 2226, **F** 332 9631, www.channings.co.uk *Map 3, G2, p250* 48 rooms. Cosy and stylish sister hotel to The Howard. Formed from five Edwardian townhouses, with great views from the top floor of Fettes, erstwhile school of James Bond and Tony Blair. Appropriately enough, there's a friendly, clubby feel to the place. Its chic brasserie is also highly rated.

B Seven Danube Street, 7 Danube St, **T** 332 2755, **F** 343 3648, seven.danubestreet@virgin.net *Map 3, G4, p250* Three en suite rooms. Exceptional, award-winning B&B in a salubrious part of town. Big and airy rooms, despite being in the basement; double and twin have four-poster beds. Unusually, the single is the same price per head. Nice touches such as shortbread, decaff coffee, dental floss and needle and thread in every room, which sums up the extreme generosity of the hostess, Fiona. Breakfast is also a cut above the rest. They have a self-contained basement flat round the corner which sleeps up to six. As with everywhere else in the New Town, parking is an issue. Booking essential.

B 19 St Bernard's Crescent, 19 St Bernard's Cres, **T/F** 332 6162, balfourwm@aol.com *Map 3, G3, p250* Two rooms. Elegant Georgian neoclassical townhouse in a magnificent sweeping crescent designed by James Milne for the son of Sir Henry Raeburn, the famous portrait painter. Grand Doric columns lead into a sumptuous interior which is more like a stately home than a B&B. Beautiful, spacious rooms, one with a William IV four-poster bed. Antiques and artwork are everywhere but it still feels homely, thanks to nice touches such as a decanter of sherry in the room, and the genial and engaging host. Breakfast more than lives up to the surroundings and is an event in itself. Minimum two nights stay. Booking essential.

C Ashlyn Guest House, 42 Inverleith Row, **T/F** 552 2954, reservations@ashlyn-edinburgh.com *Map 3, B5, p250* Elegant Georgian townhouse with interior furnishings to match. Also residents' lounge. Good location close to Botanic Garden, handy for buses to and from town, and on-street parking.

C Six Mary's Place, 6 Mary's Pl, Raeburn Pl, **T** 332 8965, **F** 624 7060, info@sixmarysplace.co.uk *Map 3, F3, p250* Eight rooms. Non-smoking guesthouse on busy Stockbridge street. Handy for neighbourhood shops and restaurants. Friendly, informal atmosphere. Offers good vegetarian cooking. Internet access in rooms.

Serviced apartments

B Canon Court Apartments, 20 Canonmills, **T** 474 7000, **F** 474 7001, www.canoncourt.co.uk *Map 3, E6, p250* Modern complex of 43 one- and two-bedroom apartments within walking distance of the New Town, Stockbridge and very close to the Botanic Garden. All fully equipped and furnished, with direct telephone line, cable TV, CD player and secure parking. Heating, linen and maid service costs included. Business facilities available.

West Edinburgh

Hotels, guesthouses and B&Bs

L The Bonham, 35 Drumsheugh Gdns, **T** 226 6050, **F** 226 6080, www.thebonham.com *Map 4, A9, p253* 48 rooms. This trio of Victorian townhouses was turned into a hotel in 1998. Rooms are all decorated individually in cool, yet elegant contemporary styles. The suites have lofty ceilings and the baths and four-poster beds are so big you could get lost in them. The superb restaurant serves Scottish cuisine with an international twist.

L Caledonian Hilton Hotel, Princes St, **T** 459 9988, **F** 225 6632, www.hilton.com *Map 4, B10, p253* 249 rooms. Prestigious, luxurious and salubrious, this West End institution underwent a recent multi-million pound refurbishment and now includes a sports club (open to the public). Its expensive main restaurant, The Pompadour, is still a great culinary experience but has lost something of its former glory. Brasserie and popular bar on ground floor.

L Norton House Hotel, Ingliston, **T** 333 1275, **F** 333 5305, nortonhouse@arcadianhotels.co.uk 47 rooms. Victorian country house set in 55 acres of parkland and only one mile from the airport. Comfortable and friendly and has a good restaurant. Also offers archery and clay pigeon shooting.

L Sheraton Grand Hotel, 1 Festival Sq, **T** 229 9131, **F** 228 4510, www.sheraton.com/grandedinburgh *Map 4, C11, p253* 261 rooms. Enormous business hotel with few aesthetic qualities, but since the creation of The Exchange it has become less incongruous. Very central and with excellent facilities and service. Some rooms have great views of the Castle. Their Grill Room restaurant is highly acclaimed and the equally acclaimed Santini (see p161) is on its doorstep. The new One Spa is the best in the city and the ultimate in pampering (see p212).

A **Hilton Edinburgh Airport**, **T** 519 4400, res.manager@ edinairport.stakis.co.uk 150 en suite rooms. So close to the airport you might confuse reception with the check-in desk. Bit pricey for what it is, but if you've time you can make use of their health and fitness club.

A **Best Western Edinburgh City**, 79 Lauriston Pl, **T** 622 7979, **F** 622 7900, www.bestwesternedinburghcity.co.uk *Map 4, D12, p253* 52 en suite rooms. Former maternity hospital, now a clean, spacious, no-frills chain hotel offering very good value and nicely placed on the fringes of the Old Town and West End. Restaurant and bar. Access for wheelchair users.

A **Melvin House Hotel**, 3 Rothesay Terr, **T** 225 5084, **F** 226 5085, www.melvinhouse.co.uk *Map 4, A8, p253* 22 en suite rooms. Charming and wonderfully atmospheric Victorian townhouse with many period features, though the rooms don't live up to the grandeur of the public areas. Well-situated in a quiet street close to the West End and Dean Village. Good value.

A **Ramada Jarvis Ellersley Country House Hotel**, Ellersley Rd, Murrayfield, **T** 337 6888, **F** 313 2543, www.ramadahotels.com *Map 4, C1, p252* 57 en suite rooms. Edwardian country house hotel only five minutes' drive from Princes Street on the way to the airport. Quiet, with plenty of rural charm and atmosphere for those who want to be far from the madding crowds.

A-B Greens Hotel, 24 Eglinton Cres, **T** 337 1565, **F** 346 2990, greens@british-trust-hotels.com *Map 4, B7, p253* 55 en suite rooms. Four linked Georgian townhouses recently restored and upgraded. Spacious and well-equipped rooms, with lift. In a quiet residential street yet handy for Haymarket and the West End.

B Point Hotel, 34 Bread St, **T** 221 5555, **F** 221 9929, www.point-hotel.co.uk *Map 4, C11, p253* 140 en suite rooms. This former Co-op department store has been stylishly refurbished and is now a paradigm of Central European chic and minimalist elegance. The suites are huge and some have jacuzzis, and some of the rooms at the front have Castle views. Handily placed for the Castle and Royal Mile. Its ground-floor restaurant offers high-quality bistro food, and the bar and grill, Mondobbo, is equally stylish, see p181. Great value for such designer style.

B-C The Original Raj, 6 West Coates, **T** 346 1333, **F** 337 6688, originalrajhotel@aol.com *Map 4, C5, p252* 17 rooms. A mile from Princes Street on the airport road. Indian theme hotel, which is immediately apparent from the large white elephants guarding the entrance. Indian furniture and soft furnishings grace the airy, spacious rooms. The overall feel is exotic yet modern and not OTT. The suites are a bit more expensive but very large and good value. The Maharaja Suite has been occupied by an A-Z list of celebs, from Shakira down to Shaking Stevens. Staff are friendly and accommodating. No car park, but being this far out of town street parking is not a great problem.

B-C 16 Lynedoch Place, 16 Lynedoch Pl, **T** 225 5507, **F** 226 4185, www.16lynedochplace.co.uk *Map 4, A9, p253* Three rooms. Great location between the West End and New Town, though parking might be an issue. Lovely Georgian townhouse with a double, twin and single room, plus small sitting room for guests. Excellent breakfast and hospitality sets it apart from the competition.

E Travel Inn, 1 Morrison Link, **T** 228 9819, **F** 228 9836, www.travelinn.co.uk *Map 4, D9, p253* 128 en suite rooms. Huge, converted office block offering the kind of facilities you get at motorway service stations. Not pretty, but to secure a bed at this price in the city centre requires sacrificing a few frills. Some rooms adapted for wheelchair users. Parking.

Hostels

E-F Belford Hostel, 6-8 Douglas Gdns, **T** 225 6209, **F** 477 4636, info@hoppo.com *Map 4, A8, p253* 98 beds in small dorms (**F**), also double rooms (**E**). Huge red sandstone ecclesiastical edifice about a mile from the West End near Dean Village and the Gallery of Modern Art. Plenty of entertainment and facilities and no curfew. It may be a converted church, but don't expect any quiet reflection.

F Eglinton Youth Hostel, 18 Eglinton Cres, **T** 337 1120, **F** 313 2053, www.syha.org.uk *Map 4, B8, p253* SYHA hostel in a quiet street about a mile west of the centre, near Haymarket train station. 160 beds, most in dorms but also 12 rooms for four. Includes continental breakfast. Doors close at 0200.

F Princes Street West Backpackers, 3-4 Queensferry St, **T/F** 226 2939, princes.west@cableinet.co.uk *Map 4, B10, p253* 40 beds in dorms, three doubles and five triples. Bar, cable TV and email facilities. Also free Sunday dinner and the seventh consecutive night is free.

Campsites

E-F Edinburgh Caravan Club Site, Marine Dr, **T** 312 6874, www.caravanclub.co.uk *Take a 14 bus from town. Map 1, p247* Open all year. 200 pitches. Run by the Caravan Club of Great Britain. Good facilities. Five miles east of the centre.

South Edinburgh

Hotels, guesthouses and B&Bs

L Prestonfield House Hotel, Priestfield Rd, **T** 668 3346, **F** 668 3976, www.prestonfieldhouse.com *Map 5, G10, p255* 31 rooms. Magnificent 17th-century mansion with period features, set in its own 13 acres of gardens below Arthur's Seat, with Highland cattle and peacocks strutting around. All this only five minutes from Princes Street. The expensive restaurant is not the best around by any means, but dining here is something special.

L Bruntsfield Hotel, 69 Bruntsfield Pl, **T** 229 1393, **F** 229 5634, www.thebruntsfield.co.uk *Map 4, F11, p253* 75 en suite rooms. Large, comfortable hotel in a quiet area overlooking Bruntsfield Links, one mile south of Princes Street. Its restaurant, The Potting Shed, serves excellent modern Scottish cuisine.

B Aries Guest House, 5 Upper Gilmour Pl, **T** 229 4669. *Map 4, E11, p253* Five rooms. Gay friendly guesthouse in a quiet street minutes from Lothian Road and the King's Theatre.

B Borough, 72-80 Causewayside, **T** 668 2255, **F** 667 6622, www.edin-borough.co.uk *Map 5, F4, p254* Nine rooms. Former snooker hall, converted into über-hip hotel-restaurant combo, designed by the same bloke who did the Hacienda in Manchester. Somehow falls short of expectations, with rooms a bit functional and the whole place already a bit frayed at the edges. Though bijoux, the rooms are comfy and come with DVD and cable. Restaurant and bar downstairs are stylish places to hang out and enjoy a cocktail or some fine food.

B-C **Ben Doran**, 11 Mayfield Gdns, **T** 667 8488, **F** 667 0076, www.ben-doran.com *Map 5, H6, p254* 10 rooms, six en suite. Lovely and relaxing place to stay in the heart of guesthouse-land. This one stands out for the warm hospitality.

C-D **Edinburgh First**, University of Edinburgh, 18 Holyrood Rd, **T** 651 2007, **F** 667 7271, www.edinburghfirst.com *Map 5, F8, p255* 800 single rooms, 120 doubles, 475 en suite. Open March-April and June-September. Massive student residence block offering functional but decent and good value accommodation. Overlooked by Arthur's Seat and handy for the Old Town and Southside. Free parking. Another 500 rooms are opening at Chancellor's Court some time in 2003.

C-D **International Guest House**, 37 Mayfield Gdns, **T** 667 2511, **F** 667 1112, intergh@easynet.co.uk *Map 5, H6, p254* Nine en suite rooms. Nicely decorated rooms, good breakfasts and warm hospitality make this a superior guesthouse.

C-D **Teviotdale House Hotel**, 53 Grange Loan, **T** 667 4376, teviotdale.house@btinternet.com *Map 5, H5, p254* Seven rooms, five en suite. No smoking. Victorian townhouse offering quiet refinement and wonderful breakfasts. Some rooms have four-poster beds. Great value.

C-D **The Town House**, 65 Gilmore Pl, **T** 229 1985, www.the townhouse.com *Map 4, E10, p253* Five en suite rooms. No smoking. Former Victorian manse retaining many of the original features. Nicely furnished rooms and guest lounge. Stands out in a street full of similar accommodation.

D **The Greenhouse**, 14 Hartington Gdns, **T** 622 7634, www.greenhouse-edinburgh.com *Map 4, F10, p253* Six rooms. Closed November-February, except New Year. No smoking. Very comfortable and friendly award-winning vegetarian/vegan guest-house on a quiet street. The breakfasts are superb and, as they rightly state, a breath of fresh air after so much of the standard artery-clogging fare. Minimum two nights stay. Booking essential.

D Rimswell House Hotel, 33 Mayfield Gdns, **T** 667 5851. www.rimswellhouse.co.uk *Map 5, H6, p254* Nine rooms, mostly en suite. Small gay-friendly hotel.

Hostels

F Argyle Backpackers Hotel, 14 Argyle Pl, **T** 667 9991, **F** 662 0002, www.argylebackpackers.co.uk *Map 5, F2, p254* 12 dorms, six double and seven triples. Located on a quiet residential street in the heart of studenty Marchmont.

F Bruntsfield Youth Hostel, 7 Bruntsfield Cres, **T** 447 2994, www.syha.org.uk *Map 4, G11, p253* Reliable and well-run SYHA hostel in quiet area overlooking the Links, and within easy reach of the centre. Doors locked at 0200.

Campsites

F Mortonhall Caravan Park, 38 Mortonhall Gate, Frogston Rd East, **T** 664 1533, **F** 664 5387, www.meadowhead.co.uk/mortonhall *Take a 7 or 11 bus from Princes Street.* 250 pitches. Open March-January. Well-equipped site about six miles southwest of town.

Leith, Newhaven and Portobello

Hotels, guesthouses and B&Bs

L-A Malmaison Hotel, 1 Tower Pl, Leith, **T** 468 5000, **F** 468 5002, www.malmaison.com *Map 6, B8, p256* 101 rooms. Parking. Award-winning and ever-expanding designer hotel in Leith's waterfront quarter, still providing the benchmark for urban style. Rooms are the epitome of sleek sophistication and cool, contemporary chic with CD in every room (good selection at reception). Suites at front are the most expensive but have the best views. Stylish brasserie and café-bar on ground floor.

C Portobello Guest House, 2 Pittville St, Portobello, **T** 669 6067. www.portobelloguesthouse.co.uk *Map 1, p247* Six rooms. Gay-friendly guesthouse by the sea, 20 minutes by bus from the city centre.

C-D Express by Holiday Inn Edinburgh-Leith, Ocean Dr, Leith, **T** 555 4422, **F** 555 4646, www.hiex-edinburgh.com *Map 6, B6, p256* 150 en suite rooms. Another huge bed factory, this one is directly opposite Ocean Terminal and Britannia, and a short walk from Leith's Shore. All the usual facilities and services, plus rooms for disabled, and under 19s go free. Good bus service to and from the city centre.

E Bar Java, 48-50 Constitution St, Leith, **T** 553 2020, www.javabedandbreakfast.co.uk *Map 6, C8, p256* 10 rooms. Basic but cheap accommodation behind this popular little bar. Set around courtyard beer garden so not ideal for early risers. Busy during the Festival and Hogmanay.

Edinburgh has a wide range of culinary options, everything from Creole to Cantonese. Scottish cuisine is also well represented, from traditional fare to more contemporary eclectic cuisine using various international influences, but always using the very best of Scottish ingredients. More and more restaurants, however, are moving away from national culinary boundaries and offering a wide range of international dishes and flavours, so you'll often find Latin American, Oriental and Pacific Rim dishes all on the same menu. This is particularly the case in the many continental-style bistros, brasseries and café-bars, which offer a more informal alternative to traditional restaurants. Most of the upmarket restaurants are in the New Town, though there are also some excellent places to be found around the 'haggis belt' (the Royal Mile) and in Leith, with its many fish restaurants and bistros located around the refurbished dockside. The area around the University campus, in Southside, is where you'll find the best-value eating in town, especially for vegetarians.

£

Price

Eating codes

£££	£20 and over
£££	
££	£11-20
£	£10 and under

Prices are based on a two-course meal for one without drinks or tips.

Most of the restaurants serve from 1200-1430 and 1800-2200 and are closed on Sundays. The exceptions are Indian, Chinese and Thai restaurants or the many excellent bistros and brasseries, many of which serve food daily until around 0100. Note that a seat in one of the more upmarket restaurants can be hard to come by during busy periods, such as the Festival, so it's best to book whenever possible. For a cheap meal, your best bet is a bar or café. The best value is often at lunchtime, when many restaurants offer two- and three-course set lunches for less than £10. Also good value are the pre-theatre dinners offered by many restaurants. These are usually available from around 1730-1800 till 1900-1930. BYOB is a commonly used abbreviation meaning bring your own bottle.

Old Town

Restaurants, bistros, bars and brasseries

£££ **The Grain Store**, 30 Victoria St, **T** 225 7635. *Mon-Thu 1200-1400, 1800-2200; Fri and Sat 1200-1500, 1800-2300; Sun 1200-1500, 1800-2200. Map 2, F3, p248* High quality Scottish ingredients served with effortless aplomb and a smile to boot. Exuberant menu features fish, game and meat, including such mouth-watering classics as carpaccio of beef. Wide selection of less orthodox starters which can be eaten combined with each other, tapas-style. The excellent cheese board is supplied by the peerless Ian Mellis, the cheesemonger, who resides below. The fabulous flavours are equalled by the attentive service and relaxed ambience. Two-course lunch only £8 and dinner £15. A real find, and popular with those in the know.

£££ Iggs, 15 Jeffrey St, **T** 557 8184. *Mon-Sat 1200-1430, 1800-2230. Closed Sun. Map 2, E7, p249* Superb Spanish restaurant with a formidable reputation amongst the city's culinary cognoscenti. Combines the flavour of the Mediterranean with contemporary Scottish cuisine. Very good wine list. Excellent tapas at lunch, though you may be better off trying the cheaper tapas bar, *Barioja*, next door (Monday-Saturday 1100-2400).

£££ La Garrigue, 31 Jeffrey St, **T** 557 3032. *Tue-Sat 1200-1430, 1830-2230; Sun 1200-1430. Map 2, D7, p249* Welcome addition to the city's already considerable stable of French culinary flair. Brings a touch of understated, lazy Languedoc to the Scottish capital, in light and airy surroundings. Simple dishes brought to the table with subtle touches that elevate the experience from the good to the memorable. Very popular so best to book. Lunch is great value.

£££ Off the Wall, 105 High St, **T** 558 1497. *Mon-Sat 1200-1400, 1730-2200. Closed Sun. Map 2, E7, p249* A sign by the entrance proclaims Off the Wall to be a 'Scottish Restaurant' but it's far more cosmopolitan than that. What it does do, in common with many of the city's best eateries, is combine the finest Scottish produce with flair and imagination, so the fillet of beef with soft braised fennel and crisp Parma ham is tender and pink (as all good Scottish beef must be). Vegetarians are also well-catered for and the puddings are luscious in the extreme. The wine list is upmarket but with low mark-up. Great value set lunch for £15. Though it's on the main drag it's not hyped, so never gets too busy.

£££ **Plaisir du Chocolat**, 251-253 Canongate, **T** 556 9524. *Tue, Wed and Sun 1000-1800, Thu-Sat 1000-2230. No smoking. Map 2, E8, p249* A rare find, this place is a slice of genuine Gallic gastronomic greatness. Not content to be one of the city's best French restaurants, it is also its finest tearoom, offering some 180 varieties of tea, hot chocolate, cakes and biscuits, sandwiches, brioche and petit fours. They also do a fine French *petit-déjeuner*, high tea and a wonderful (but not cheap at £15) weekend brunch. Now open in the evenings at weekends when the menu includes such classics as tarte tatin, fondue and superb foie gras. Their bread, which is *magnifique* and worth the trip alone, is for sale in the *épicerie* across the road, along with the many other tastebud temptations.

£££ **The Tower**, Museum of Scotland, Chambers St, **T** 225 3003. *Daily 1200-2300. No smoking. Map 2, H4, p248* Still the place to be seen among the corporate set, the superb Scottish menu and magnificent views across the city skyline from the rooftop terrace are hard to beat. This is modern dining at its sophisticated best.

£££ **The Witchery by the Castle**, 352 Castlehill, **T** 225 5613. *Daily 1200-1600, 1730-2330. Map 2, F2, p248* Dining doesn't get more atmospheric than this. The Witchery's reputation has spread far and wide and it is frequented by the likes of Jack Nicholson and Michael Douglas. But though eating here is more of a life experience than simply a meal, style does not take precedence over content, and established favourites such as roast breast of wild mallard with a warm endive and orange salad or seared sea bream with pumpkin and potato rösti and rosemary cream are flavoursome and served with aplomb. The wine list is phenomenal, with over 900 available. Downstairs, in a converted schoolyard, is the impossibly romantic Secret Garden, which shares the same glorious Scottish menu. Impecunious souls who wish to savour the atmosphere can plump for the two-course set lunch or pre-theatre supper at under £10.

££ Bann UK, 5 Hunter Sq, **T** 226 1112. *Daily 1100-2300. Map 2, F6, p248* Bann's is still one the city's leading vegetarian eateries with an effortlessly cool, minimalist look and a lifestyle menu to match. They offer an imaginative and adventurous range of dishes, taking veggie food far away from the tedious, sandal-wearing days of old. This is a popular street performing venue during the Festival, so great for an al fresco lunch, if that's your cup of herbal tea. Busy but laid-back and generally good value.

££ Black Bo's, 57-61 Blackfriars St, **T** 557 6136. *Sun-Thu 1800-2230, Fri-Sat 1200-1400, 1800-2230. Bar open 1630-0100. Map 2, F7, p249* Vegetarian restaurant with bar next door serving the same food. One of the city's great culinary experiences, though not cheap, and so good even the most fanatical carnivore might be tempted to give up meat. Supremely imaginative use of various fruits gives the exotically delicious dishes a real splash of colour.

££ Creelers, 3 Hunter Sq, **T** 220 4447. *Sun, Mon and Thu 1200-1400, 1700-2230; Tue-Wed 1200-1400 (May-Oct only), 1700-2230; Fri-Sat 1200-1400, 1700-2300. No smoking. Map 2, E6, p248* From the owners of the famous Arran restaurant and smokehouse, the capital version serves the same wonderfully fresh seafood, with outdoor seating in the summer. Highlights include the sensational smoked or cured salmon and lip-smacking langoustines grilled in garlic butter.

££ The Dial, 44-46 George IV Bridge, **T** 225 7179. *Mon-Sat 1200-1500, 1800-2300, Sun 1200-1500, 1900-2300. Map 2, G4, p248* Basement restaurant that's as notable for its cool design as for its top-notch modern Scottish cuisine. Menu features some old favourites as well as more unusual Caledonian culinary incarnations, and more than just a token veggie selection. Superb-value two-course lunch for £6.95.

★ Pre-theatre dining deals

Best

- La Café St Honoré, p152
- Maison Bleue, p146
- Petit Paris, p147
- The Witchery by the Castle, p143

££ **Doric Tavern**, 15/16 Market St, **T** 225 1084. *Mon-Sat 1200-2230, Sun 1230-2230 (Apr-Oct only). Bar open Mon-Sat 1200-0100, Sun 1230-2400. Map 2, E5, p248* Opposite Waverley Station, this upstairs bistro is an Edinburgh institution. It can get very busy, which isn't surprising given the mouth-watering Scottish menu and attention to detail. The set menus are excellent value. Wine bar next door is heaving after working hours.

££ **Dubh Prais**, 123b High St, **T** 557 5732. *Tue-Sat 1200-1400, 1830-2230. Map 2, E6, p248* Pronounced "doo prash", this tiny basement restaurant in the heart of the Royal Mile offers the best of traditional Scottish cooking, as well as more contemporary innovations. Dinner is à la carte, but you can enjoy a two-course set lunch for a tenner. Chef/owner James McWilliams enjoys a huge and loyal local following, which says it all.

££ **Gordon's Trattoria**, 231 High St, **T** 225 7992. *Sun-Thu 1200-2400; Fri and Sat till 0300. Map 2, E5, p248* Great-value Italian food served with typical gusto at almost any time of the day or night, which is why it's so popular, and therefore cramped at lunchtimes and in the evenings. Great for people-watching in summer when tables spill out on to the street.

££ **Le Sept**, 7 Old Fishmarket Close, **T** 225 5428. *Mon-Thu 1200-1345, 1800-2200, Fri 1200-2300, Sat 1200-2230, Sun 1200-2130. Map 2, F5, p248* Down a steep, cobbled close off the High Street below St Giles. This lively little restaurant is famed for its superb crêpes, but also has a three-course set menu offering good French bistro-type food.

££ Légume, 11 South College St, **T** 667 1597. *Mon-Sat 1200-1400, 1730-2130. Map 2, H6, p248* Well-positioned just off the Bridges, this vegetarian newcomer serves up a limited but well-executed menu with a distinct French influence. Service is excellent so it's good for a fast lunchtime repast.

££ Maison Bleue, 36-38 Victoria St, **T** 226 1900. *Daily 1200-1500, 1700-late. Map 2, F3, p248* No chance of missing this bright, blue three-storey building. Inside there's a lively, Mediterranean feel reflected in the imaginative, 'anything-goes' approach to eating. Choose from *Les Bouchées* (mouthfuls), *Les Bouchées Doubles* and *Les Brochettes* which feature a wide range of French-influenced flavours, from North African to Oriental. Their BYOB policy (Sunday-Thursday), set lunch and pre-theatre menus make it even more of an appealing proposition.

££ Mamma's American Pizza Company, 30 Grassmarket, **T** 225 6464. *Sun-Thu 1000-2400, Fri/Sat till 0100. Map 2, H2, p248* Good old Italian-American serving up endless varieties of pizza with a big smile to hordes of grateful customers. None of yer fancy filled crusts here, just thin crisp pizza, as the Big Man intended. No bookings taken on Friday or Saturday night. No smoking. Also has two branches in the New Town, at 2 Broughton Place and 1 Howard Street, Canonmills.

££ Nicolsons, 6a Nicolson St, **T** 557 4567. *Mon-Sat 1200-1500, 1700-late. Map 2, H7, p249* Large, airy bistro, done out in 1930s Art Deco style and attracting an upwardly mobile crowd, as well as the occasional Harry Potter fan (JK Rowling used to come here to write when it was a humble café). Great for a bottle of wine or a martini and the food's good, too – Mediterranean-style with a Far Eastern tinge.

££ North Bridge Brasserie, 20 North Bridge, **T** 662 2900. *Daily 1215-1430, 1815-2230. Bar open Sun-Thu 1000-2300, Fri-Sat till 0100. No smoking. Map 2, E6, p248* Located in the swanky Scotsman Hotel, erstwhile home of *The Scotsman* newspaper. Worth visiting to marvel at the imaginative use of the high ceiling with a balcony running right round it, reached via a metal spiral staircases. Excellent brasserie menu features grilled meats and seafood, plus sushi and vegetarian choices, though a definite minus are the highly priced starters. Enjoy the leather couches or the view from above.

££ The Outsider, 15-16 George IV Bridge, **T** 226 3131. *Daily 1100-2300. Map 2, G4, p248* From the same team that brought you The Apartment on the Southside (see p163), this new culinary player has, unsurprisingly, quickly established a solid reputation. Individual décor and furnishings lend a classy backdrop to the main event, the food, which is tasty, filling and really good value. Lamb cutlets and merguez on couscous and skewers of roast duck, plums and onions are under a tenner. Staff are chatty, charming and attractive. Book well in advance to secure a seat.

££ Pancho Villas, 240 Canongate, **T** 557 4416. *Mon-Thu 1200-1430, 1800-2200, Fri-Sat 1200-2230, Sun 1800-2230. Map 2, E8, p249* If you want to stuff yourself on the finest Mexican food and have a good time in the process, then look no further. Clean, simple lines help create a relaxed atmosphere and the service is super-efficient. Cheaper at lunchtime, hence its popularity.

££ Petit Paris, 38-40 Grassmarket, **T** 226 2442. *Daily 1200-1500, 1730 till late. Map 2, G2, p248* Francophiles will fall in love with this place. Everything about it is French to the core, from the chequered tablecloths to the coquettish waitresses. The food is delectable and includes classic dishes such as Toulouse sausages and coq au vin. All in all, a wonderful experience, despite the squeeze. Great lunchtime bargains with a selection of mains for only £5 and pre-theatre deals. BYOB Sunday-Thursday, £2 corkage.

££ **Prego**, 38 St Mary's St, **T** 557 5754. *Tue-Sat 1200-1430, 1800-2200. Map 2, F8, p249* Tucked away out of sight just off the Royal Mile, this relaxed Italian restaurant is charming and urbane and does the simple things well, such as ossobuco alla Milanese and penne del captiano . The same à la carte menu is offered for lunch and dinner, though there are also plenty of cheaper pasta amd primi piatti options (£4-7) during the day.

££ **Suruchi**, 14a Nicolson St, **T** 556 6583. *Mon-Sat 1200-1400, 1730-2330, Sun 1730-2330. Map 2, H7, p249* Opposite the Festival Theatre. A cut above the average curry house, offering varied southern Indian cuisine with a strong vegetarian emphasis. Their set lunch and pre-theatre dinner are particularly good value at £9.95. BYOB.

££ **Viva Mexico**, 41 Cockburn St, **T** 226 5145. *Mon-Sat 1200-1400, 1800-2230, Sun 1800-2200. Map 2, E5, p248* This Mexican restaurant has been around longer than most and it's easy to see why – definitely one of the top two in town. The reliably filling food is spicy and authentic, featuring such standards as *pollo en chipolte* and rice, black beans and tortillas.

£ **Kebab Mahal**, 7 Nicolson Sq, **T** 667 5214. *Sun-Thu 1200-2400, Fri and Sat 1200-0200. Map 2, H7, p249* No frills Halal café-takeaway serving good kebabs and curries for under a fiver. You wouldn't bring a first date here or linger all night but who cares at these prices? No alcohol served on the premises. Attracts local Asian families and impecunious students in equal measure.

£ **Khushi's**, 16 Drummond St, **T** 556 8996. *Mon-Thu 1200-1430, 1700-2030, Fri/Sat till 2100. Map 2, G7, p249* The city's first ever Indian restaurant has been serving simple, tasty curries to poor students ever since India's independence. Basic decor but you can't argue with such great value. Service is speedy so good for a quick meal. Several vegetarian options. BYOB and no corkage charge.

Cafés, sandwich bars and delis

Café Hub, Castlehill, **T** 473 2015. *Sun-Mon 0930-1800; Tue-Sat 0930-2200. No smoking. Map 2, F3, p248 See also Festivals, p198* The relaxing blues and yellows of this stylish, chilled-out café provide a soothing backdrop to the tasty and inventive food. Seating outside on the terrace in summer.

Café Florentin, 8 St Giles St, **T** 225 6267. *Daily 0700-2200 (till 2100 in winter). Map 2, E4, p248* Large and lively place to stop for a coffee, a filled croissant and a generous slice of Edinburgh life. Beginning to fray at the edges a little, but a welcome antidote to the prevailing corporate blandness.

City Art Centre Café, 1 Market St, **T** 220 3359. *Mon-Sat 0900-1700, Sun (only during exhibitions) 1100-1700. No smoking. Map 2, E5, p248* Good coffee and cakes and a selection of cheap snacks and main dishes in a spacious environment with helpful staff. Good for a quick bite.

Elephant House, 21 George IV Bridge, **T** 220 5355. *Daily 0800-2300. Map 2, G4, p248* Very studenty – a great place to linger over coffee and bagels or one of many cheap snacks and main courses. Café-bar by evening with live music. Mellow vibe and lots of pachyderms but not a mahout in sight.

Best

★ **Outdoor eating and drinking**

- Café Hub, p149
- Cramond Inn, p180
- Oloroso, p152
- The Sheep Heid Inn, p151
- The Pear Tree House, p183

Elephant's Sufficiency, 170 High St, **T** 220 0666. *Mon-Fri 0800-2200; Sat and Sun 0900-2200; till 1700 in winter months. Map 2, F5, p248* Perennial favourite with locals and tourists. Great value, with a huge selection of breakfasts and lunches. It gets totally crazy at lunchtimes, so prepare to wait or try somewhere a less popular.

Favorit, 19-20 Teviot Pl, **T** 220 6880. *Daily 0830-0300. Map 5, D3, p254* Who needs New York when there are place like this? Popular with students and workers alike. Friendly, efficient service and diner-style booth seats encourage you to linger over your cappuccino or smoothie. They also do pasta dishes, wraps and sandwiches, breakfasts and beer on draught. Also at 30-32 Leven Street.

Fruitmarket Café, Fruitmarket Gallery, 45 Market St, **T** 226 1843. *Mon-Sat 1100-1700, Sun 1200-1700. No smoking. Map 2, D5, p248* One of the coolest cafés in town with windows large enough to guarantee being seen. A great place for a quick, cheap and tasty lunch, or just for coffee and a chat.

The Lower Aisle, High Kirk of St Giles, High St (entrance via the church or Parliament Square), **T** 225 5147. *Mon-Fri 0830-1630, Sun 0900-1400. Map 2, F4, p248* This self-service café in the vaults under St Giles is popular with a broad range of clients, from legal eagles to pensioners. Good for a cheap light lunch.

Arthur's Seat and Duddingston

Restaurants, bistros, bars and brasseries

££ The Sheep Heid Inn, 43 The Causeway, Duddingston, **T** 656 6951. *Mon-Wed 1100-2300; Thu-Sat till 2400; Sun 1230-2300. Food served Mon-Thu 1200-1500; Fri and Sat 1200-2100; Sun 1230-2000. Map 5, E12, p255* Great place to relax with a pint on a sunny afternoon after a walk up Arthur's Seat, which is why it's so busy, especially for their hearty Sunday lunches.

New Town

Restaurants, bistros, bars and brasseries

£££ Bellini, 8b Abercromby Pl, **T** 476 2602. *Tue-Fri 1200-1430, 1830 till late; Sat 1800 till late; Sun 1230-2100. Map 3, G7, p251* Superior Italian food served in elegant Georgian surroundings. Those who prefer a touch of sumptuous exclusivity about their dining experience take note: few know about this place save the New Town culinary cognoscenti. A great place for a slow, lingering dinner, with, friendly, attentive service. Lunchtime two-course special is a snip at £8.90.

£££ Café Royal Oyster Bar, 17a West Register St, **T** 556 4124. *Daily 1200-1400, 1900-2200. Map 2, C4, p248* An Edinburgh institution and much-loved by numerous celebrities. The ornate tiles and stained-glass windows create an atmosphere of Victorian elegance and opulence. There are better (and cheaper) seafood restaurants in town but none are as classy. The adjoining Bistro Bar is just as impressive and less damaging on the bank balance.

£££ Le Café Saint-Honoré, 34 Thistle St La, **T** 226 2211.
Mon-Fri 1200-1415, 1700-2200, Sat 1200-1415, 1800-2200.
Map 2, B1, p248 Tucked away in a little side street, this place
couldn't be any more French. An authentic corner of Paris in the
heart of Scotland's capital. The food is seriously French, too, and
seriously priced, but seriously wonderful; tender, plump meat and
game rubs shoulders with fresh and varied fish and seafood.
Excellent-value set menu served 1700-1900.

£££ Duck's at Le Marché Noir, 2-4 Eyre Pl, **T** 558 1608.
Mon-Fri 1200-1430, 1800-2230, Sat 1800-2230, Sun 1800-2130.
Map 3, F6, p250 Classic French provincial cooking married to the
best of Ecossais served with precision in sumptuous surroundings.
Perhaps Edinburgh's finest French? Complemented by an
extensive wine list.

£££ Librizzi's, 69 North Castle St, **T** 226 1155. *Mon-Sat 1200-
1400, 1730-2300.* *Map 4, A11, p253* Well-situated New Town
branch serves up mouth-watering Sicilian delicacies of a consist-
ently high standard. Fish is supreme here, from red mullet baked
with rosemary, garlic and lemon to grilled sea bass with parma
ham and mushrooms. The dessert menu makes too many offers
you simply cannot refuse.

£££ Number One, 1 Princes St, **T** 557 6727. *Mon-Thu 1200-1400,
1900-2200, Fri 1200-1400, 1900-2230, Sat 1900-2230, Sun 1900-2200.*
Map 2, C5, p248 Understated opulence situated under the
Balmoral Hotel. The muted elegance of the decor is matched by
the food, which comes with the minimum of fuss. Spacious and
discreet, so good for an intimate dinner à deux. Superb-value
lunch (£12.50 for two courses and £15.50 for three).

£££ Oloroso, 33 Castle St, **T** 226 7614. *Daily 1200-1430,
1800-2230. Bar open 1100-2300.* *Map 4, A12, p253* This relative

newcomer is a strong contender for the place to be seen around town. A lift takes you up to the cool penthouse eating space where chef Tony Singh has earned an enviable reputation for doing the simple things with style and considerable attention to detail. And then there are the memorable views of the castle and New Town. The menu leans towards contemporary Scottish and the adjacent bar serves wonderful bar snacks at a fraction of the cost. A place this good is always rammed full so book well ahead.

££ Café Marlayne, 76 Thistle St, **T** 226 2230. *Tue-Sat 1200-1400, 1800-2200. Map 2, C0, p248* This new enfant in the playground of Edinburgh French cuisine may be tiny but won't be bullied by the bigger kids. Such bijou surroundings ensure a degree of intimacy and personal service that others can only dream of. The quality of food is equally high and there's that satisfying sense of uncovering a real treasure. Booking is a must on any night of the week.

££ Est Est Est, 135a George St, **T** 225 2555. *Mon-Sat 1200-2300, Sun 1200-2230. Map 4, A12, p253* Huge, bright, buzzing Italian-style restaurant – one of a chain – serving excellent-value food in sleek, modern surroundings. Great for families but gets very busy and booking is advisable. Even Mick Jagger was turned away, proving that you can't always get what you want.

££ Forth Floor, Harvey Nichols, 11-13 South St Andrew St, **T** 524 8350. *Daily 1200-1500 and 1800-2230. Map 2, B4, p248* At last, Edinburgh's aspirational set can feel good about themselves in everyone's favourite uber-posh department store. The restaurant, on the fourth floor commands wonderful views across the Forth and though the prices seem steep the cooking does not disappoint. Seared scallops and grilled seabass are fresh as a supermodel's lipstick. The brasserie menu offers a more modest alternative.

££ **Hadrian's**, 2 North Bridge, **T** 557 5000. *Mon-Sat 0700-1030, 1200-1430, 1830-2230, Sun 0730-1100, 1230-1500, 1830-2230. Map 2, C5, p248* Round the corner from Number One (see p152), Hadrian's serves excellent modern Scottish cuisine with nouvelle-ish tendencies. The mint green and dark chocolate decor provides a cool and soothing backdrop to their superb-value fixed-price menu (£10.50 for three courses).

££ **Kweilin**, 19-21 Dundas St, **T** 557 1875. *Tue-Thu 1200-2300, Fri/Sat 1200-2400, Sun 1600-2300. Map 3, G7, p251* A bit more expensive than other Chinese restaurants in town but well worth it for some of the most imaginative Cantonese cooking around. Seafood dishes are particularly recommended.

££ **La P'tite Folie**, 61 Frederick St, **T** 225 7983. *Mon-Sat 1200-1500, 1800-2300; Sun 1800-2300. Map 2, C0, p248* Straightforward, unpretentious and authentic French bistro serving uncomplicated but tasty dishes to a grateful clientele. Menu offers more variety than most. Great value three-course lunch for £7.90 is very popular, so customers are not encouraged to linger.

££ **The Mussel Inn**, 61-65 Rose St, **T** 225 5979. *Mon-Thu 1200-1500, 1800-2200, Fri and Sat 1100-2200. Map 2, C2, p248* What could be better than a huge pot of steaming fresh mussels and a bowl of fantastic chips? Not much, judging by the popularity of this place, in the heart of pub-land. A must for seafood-lovers.

££ **Nargile**, 73 Hanover St, **T** 225 5755. *Mon-Thu 1200-1400, 1730-2230, Fri/Sat 1200-1400, 1730-2300. Map 2, B2, p248* Facing stiff competition from the plethora of eating options in the New Town, this Turkish restaurant is doing very nicely. The decor is subtle and contemporary, leaving happy diners free to concentrate on the wonderful flavours. The terminally hungry can try their famed mezze dinner.

££ Podricious…The Bistro, 192 Rose St, **T** 225 2208. *Tue-Sat 1200-1400, 1800-2200. Map 4, A11, p253* Rose Street is pedestrian in more than one sense, but this is a culinary oasis amidst a sea of run-of-the-mill stodge. Enthusiastically run by husband and wife team, the food leans towards traditional Scots, but the real stars are the succulent steaks. Excellent value and the two-course set lunch even more so at a positively parsimonious £9.

££ Ricks, 55a Frederick St, **T** 622 7800. *Daily 0700-0100. Map 4, A12, p253 See also Sleeping, p126* Of all the bars in all the towns in all the world…you really ought to walk into this one. The sleek, contemporary décor is as easy on the eye as most of the clientele, many of whom are merely here to be seen, but that doesn't detract from a very good fusion-based menu that features a nice balance of fish, crustacea and meat as well as a few vegetarian choices (spicy satay noodles with bok choy and shitake mushrooms are particularly good). Also good for a pre-prandial cocktail from their impressive list or for a big night out, especially at weekends.

££ Siam Erawan, 48 Howe St, **T** 226 3675. *Daily 1200-1430, 1800-2245. Map 3, G6, p250* Edinburgh's original Thai restaurant and still the best, according to many. The cosy basement ambience encourages you to take your time. The same people have two other branches: Erawan Express, 176 Rose Street, **T** 220 0059; and Erawan Oriental, 14 South St Andrew Street, **T** 556 4242.

££ Tapas Olé, 10 Eyre Pl, **T** 556 2754. *Sun-Thu 1100-2200, Fri/Sat 1100-2230. Map 3, F6, p250* Excellent tapas served in bright, lively and colourful surroundings. Good choices on offer and the set menu allows you to sample at least nine for £13. Also a lunch menu at £6 for six tapas. Friendly service and a good vibe but gets very busy at weekends. There's a branch in the Old Town, at 4a Forrest Road, **T** 225 7069.

££ YO! Sushi, Unit 5, Hanover Buildings, 66 Rose St, **T** 220 6040. *Daily 1200-2300. Map 2, C1, p248* New Edinburgh branch of the famous London chain brings the authentic Japanese fast food experience. All the favourites such as maki, nagiri and sashimi pass before your eyes on a giant conveyer belt in glorious technicolour. It's bright, noisy and great fun. Underneath is YO! Below, see p176.

£ Bar Napoli, 75 Hanover St, **T** 225 2600. *Daily 1130-0300. Map 2, B2, p248* Popular and great-value Italian eaterie packs 'em in all hours of the night and day (well, almost). Huge space and menu to match. Their set lunch is cheap as chips.

£ Henderson's Salad Table, 94 Hanover St, **T** 225 2131. *Mon-Sat 0800-2230. Map 2, B1, p248* This basement vegetarian self-service restaurant is the oldest in the city and still one of the best. It can get very busy but manages to combine efficiency with comfort. Excellent-value two-course set lunch. Upstairs is their deli and takeaway and round the corner is *Henderson's Bistro*, which provides the same excellent food but in more intimate surroundings, with table service and at only slightly higher prices.

Cafés, sandwich bars and delis

Glass & Thompson, 2 Dundas St, **T** 557 0909. *Mon-Sat 0830-1730, Sun 1100-1630. No smoking. Map 2, A1, p248* Coffee shop and deli with the emphasis on quality food. Popular with local residents who know a good thing when they see it.

The Queen Street Café, The Scottish National Portrait Gallery, 1 Queen St, **T** 557 2844. *Mon-Sat 1000-1630, Sun 1200-1630. No smoking. Map 2, A3, p248* The best scones and caramel shortcake in town, not to mention excellent-value snacks and light meals, served in grand surroundings.

Calton Hill and Broughton

Restaurants, bistros, bars and brasseries

£££ Haldane's, 39 Albany St, **T** 556 8407. *Mon-Fri 1200-1300 (bookings only), 1800-2130, Sat-Sun 1800-2130.* *Map 3, G8, p251* Smart Scottish country house cuisine only a stone's throw from the buzz of Broughton. Excellent-value set lunch.

££ Café Mediterraneo, 73 Broughton St, **T** 557 6900. *Mon-Thu 0800-1800, Fri/Sat 0800-2000.* *Map 3, G9, p251* The fairly unassuming little deli out front gives no indication of the excellent dishes on offer in the small, bright restaurant behind. Cooking, not surprisingly, is Mediterranean-influenced with an imaginative twist, very filling and amazingly good value. Good place for breakfast. Book ahead for dinner.

££ The Lost Sock Diner, 11 East London St, **T** 557 6097. *Mon 0900-1600, Tue-Fri 0900-2200, Sat 1000-2200, Sun 1100-1700.* *Map 3, F9, p251* Laundrettes can be pretty enervating places at the best of times, but someone here has hit on the bright idea of attaching a cool, retro American-style diner to the one at the bottom of Broughton Street. Huge selection of snacks, wraps, breakfasts, burgers etc by day and at night the menu becomes a bit more sophisticated, but still great value. Great place to relax with the newspaper while you wait for your smalls to dry.

££ Tapas Tree, 1 Forth St, **T** 556 7718. *Daily 1100-2300.* *Map 3, G9, p251* This Spanish restaurant has built up a reputation for excellent food and service. Their tapas are good value, particularly the lunchtime specials, and they even offer a vegetarian selection. Flamenco on Thursday nights. Booking advised at weekends.

Cafés, sandwich bars and delis

Embo, 29 Haddington Pl, Leith Walk, **T** 652 3880. *Mon-Fri 0730-1530, Sat 0900-1630. Map 3, F10, p251* Part deli, part art gallery, this place is just gorgeous. Great coffee, great Italian panini and a cool vibe. We just wish it would stay open a bit later.

Valvona & Crolla, 19 Elm Row, **T** 556 6066. *Mon-Sat 0800-1800. No smoking. Map 3, F10, p251* The deli out front is more authentically Italian than almost anything you'd find in New York, and is worth browsing before you head through to the café at the rear. Great home cooking and the best capuccino in town. The perfect place for a big Saturday brunch. Needless to say, somewhere this good is very popular.

Stockbridge and Inverleith

Restaurants, bistros, bars and brasseries

££ Bell's Diner, 7 St Stephen St, **T** 225 8116. *Sun-Fri 1800-2230, Sat 1200-2230. Map 3, G5, p250* This is where the good burghers of Stockbridge come for the best burgers in town. Popular with locals, students and tourists alike who come for its honest, filling and great-value food in an informal atmosphere.

££ Howies, 4-6 Glanville Pl, **T** 225 5553. *Daily 1200-1430, 1800-2230. Map 3, G4, p250* Something of an Edinburgh institution, this chain of bistros hits the spot every time with imaginative Scottish food that is always tasty and great value (BYOB policy), in an informal atmosphere. The others are at 29 Waterloo Place, 208 Bruntsfield Place, and 10-14 Victoria Street.

★ **Weekend brunch**

ᗺ •Café Mediterraneo, p157
ⅇ •Maxi's, p159
﬩ •Hadrian's Brasserie, p154
ﬨ •Kaffee Politik, p165
  •Valvona & Crolla, p158

££ Loon Fung, 2 Warriston Pl, **T** 556 1781. *Mon-Fri 1200-2400, Sat 1400-0100, Sun 1400-2400. Map 3, E6, p250* Still one of the great Oriental eating experiences in town, this Cantonese restaurant is an old favourite, with a wide selection of dim sum and seafood dishes. The surroundings are less than plush but it's the food that counts here.

Cafés, sandwich bars and delis

Au Gourmand, 1 Brandon Terr, **T** 624 4666. *Mon-Sat 0900-1800, Sun 1000-1700. Map 3, E6, p250* This great little neighbourhood French deli/café is an absolute must if you're in the area, whether it's to stop off for some tasty French cheese or charcuterie and delicious home-baked bread for a picnic in the Botanics, or to sit in and sample their sweet and savoury crêpes.

Maxi's, 33 Raeburn Pl, **T** 343 3007. *Mon 0830-1900, Tue-Sat 0830-2300, Sun 1000-1800. Map 3, F4, p250* Café/deli with an Italian emphasis. Good, healthy eating and everything as fresh as new-cut grass. Great place for breakfast or brunch, but also evening menu on offer. The best cheap eating in Stockbridge.

Terrace Café, Royal Botanic Garden, Inverleith Row, **T** 552 0616. *Daily 0930-1730 (1530 in winter). No smoking. Map 3, D4, p250* Set in the grounds next to Inverleith House, this basic little self-service café holds few surprises, but the views of the Castle, Old Town and Arthur's Seat take some beating.

West Edinburgh

Restaurants, bistros, bars and brasseries

£££ **The Atrium**, 10 Cambridge St (same building as the Traverse Theatre), **T** 228 8882. *Mon-Fri 1200-1400, 1800-2200, Sat 1800-2200. Map 4, C11, p253* Award-winning Scottish cooking in elegant modern surroundings. This outstanding restaurant is one of the best in town, but by no means the most expensive.

£££ **Scalini**, 10 Melville Pl, Queensferry St, **T** 220 2999. *Mon-Sat 1200-1430, 1800-2200. No smoking. Map 4, A10, p253* Intimate Italian boasting a range of more sophisticated dishes and wines that sets it apart from most others. Expensive within this food category but the personal touch makes it worth every cent.

£££ **Stac Polly**, 8-10 Grindlay St, **T** 229 5405. *Mon-Fri 1200-1430, 1800-2200, Sat/Sun 1800-2200. Map 4, C11, p253* Elegant Scottish restaurant famous for its now legendary haggis in filo pastry, as well as numerous other mouth-watering native dishes with a gallic touch. Also has a subterranean sister at 29-33 Dublin Street.

££ **blue**, 10 Cambridge St, **T** 221 1222. *Mon-Sat 1200-1500, 1800-2300. Bar Mon-Thu 1130-2400, Fri/Sat 1130-0100. Map 4, C11, p253* The stylish and minimalist interior of this leading city bistro attracts the arty and media types as well as the more sober suits. Sister to the outstanding Atrium, so not surprisingly the food on offer is a substantial cut above the rest. Its well-stocked bar boasts a satisfying selection of malts, and excellent service.

★ Late-night eating

££ French Corner Bistro, 17 Queensferry St, **T** 226 1890.
Mon-Thu 1200-1500, 1700-2200, Fri till 2230, Sat 1200-1600, 1700-2300. Map 4, A10, p253 Genuinely different French bistro food served by very willing waiting staff. Superb-value two-course lunch for £6.90 and dinner for under £15.

££ Jasmine Chinese Restaurant, 32 Grindlay St, **T** 229 5757.
Mon-Thu 1200-1400, 1700-2330, Fri till 0030, Sat 1400-0030, Sun 1400-2330. Map 4, C11, p253 Handy for the theatres and cinemas, this stylish and modern Chinese restaurant is better value than most, and something a little bit different.

££ Rogue, Scottish Widows Building, 67 Morrison St, **T** 228 2700.
Mon-Sat 1200-1500, 1800-2300. Map 4, C10, p253 David Ramsden, formerly of (fitz)Henry in Leith, has moved into the city's burgeoning financial district with this cool, stylish bar-restaurant. Eating here is not so much a meal as a cinematic experience, directed by Fellini. You can pretty much have what you want, from a relatively humble tangy Thai chicken soup and shredded duck sandwich with pickled cucumber right up to a more extravagant grilled west coast lobster with asparagus and black truffle salad.

££ Santini, 8 Conference Sq, **T** 221 7788. *Mon-Fri 1200-1430, 1830-2230, Sat 1830-2230. Bar Mon-Fri 1200-1500, 1700-2400, Sat 1700-2400. Map 4, C11, p253* With such a sleek, chic interior, this is the smartest Italian restaurant in town. With two branches in

London and one in Milan, Mr Santini knows how to wow the punters. Everything is cooked to perfection. The bistro, Santini Bis, is more informal with its own menu.

££ Shamiana, 14 Brougham St, **T** 228 2265. *Mon-Thu 1800-2100, Fri-Sat 1800-2130, Sun 1800-2000. Map 4, D12, p253* Nothing fancy to look at but a greet wee Indian restaurant. Its reputation has spread far and wide which is why it's essential to book a table in advance, especially given the limited opening hours.

£ La Cuisine D'Odile, 13 Randolph Cres, **T** 225 5685. *Tue-Sat 1200-1400 only. Map 4, A10, p253* Hidden away in the French Institute, this is a real find. Genuine quality French cuisine at amazingly low prices. Great views from the terrace in the summer.

Cafés, sandwich bars and delis

The Gallery Café, The Scottish Gallery of Modern Art, 74 Belford Rd, **T** 332 8600. *Mon-Sat 1000-1630, Sun 1400-1630. No smoking. Map 4, A6, p253* There are few better ways to spend a couple of hours on a sunny afternoon than to sit outside in the walled sculpture garden enjoying coffee and cakes, a light snack, or something more substantial washed down with a glass of wine. This is one of the city's great delights.

Ndbele, 57 Home St, **T** 221 1141. *Daily 1000-2200. Map 4, E11/12, p253* A real taste of southern Africa in Tollcross. Huge selection of filling sandwiches with some unusual fillings such as smoked ostrich. Friendly atmosphere.

Two Thin Laddies, 103 High Riggs, **T** 229 0653. *Daily 0800-1900. Map 4, D12, p253* It's a sandwich bar but not as we know it. The food here is totally original and healthy and the cakes are scrummy, too. Apparently one thin laddie has gone, leaving the other to keep up the legendary banter all by himself. The original, and much smaller, shop is at 6 Grassmarket.

South Edinburgh

Restaurants, bistros, bars and brasseries

££ Ann Purna, 45 St Patrick's Sq, **T** 662 1807. *Mon-Fri 1200-1400, 1730-2230, Sat/Sun 1730-2230. No smoking. Map 5, D4, p254* Well-respected vegetarian/vegan restaurant specializing in southern Indian and Gujarati cooking. Understated elegance and great value.

££ The Apartment, 7-13 Barclay Pl, **T** 228 6456. *Mon-Fri 1800-2300, Sat/Sun 1200-1500, 1800-2300. Map 4, F11, p253* Hip and happening place where the portions are as big as the owner's personality. A truly different eating experience with dishes divided into 'CHL' s (Chunky Healthy Lines), 'Slabs', 'Fish Things' and 'Other Things'. All in all, a great night out.

££ Blonde, 75 St Leonard's St, **T** 668 2917. *Mon 1800-2200, Tue-Sun 1200-1430, 1800-2200. Map 4, F11, p253* Formerly one of the Howie's chain this new venture continues to get it right. Good range of well-prepared, and generously-proportioned, dishes brought to the table by efficient and attentive waiting staff. All in all, a relaxed and pleasurable experience.

££ Buffalo Grill, 12-14 Chapel St, **T** 667 7427. *Mon-Fri 1200-1400, 1800-2215, Sat 1800-2215, Sun 1700-2200. Map 5, D4, p254* This is beef central. The steaks are high quality and limitless in this small and intimate diner decked out in Wild West style. It's not all burgers and steaks, but that's why people keep coming. Also at 1 Raeburn Place in Stockbridge.

££ **Kalpna**, 2-3 St Patrick's Sq, **T** 667 9890. *Mon-Fri 1200-1400, 1730-2300, Sat 1730-2300. No smoking. Map 5, D4, p254* This popular and imaginative Indian vegetarian is one of the best of its kind in the country, using fantastically inventive and sophisticated sauces. Buffet lunch is a bargain but not quite the same as the full dinner experience.

££ **The Marque**, 19-21 Causewayside, **T** 466 6660. *Tue-Thu 1200-1400, 1800-2200, Fri till 2300, Sat 1230-1400, 1800-2300, Sun till 2200. No smoking. Map 5, F5, p254* Converted from three old antique shops, the food on offer displays the same quirky creativity as the interior design. The chef, formerly of the highly acclaimed Atrium, thinks nothing of spicing up a battered cod fillet with cumin, and it's these innovative touches that make eating here a memorable experience. Has a sister restaurant, Marque Central, in Grindlay Street, which does a good pre-theatre menu.

££ **Sweet Melinda's**, 11 Roseneath St, **T** 229 7953. *Tue-Sat 1200-1400, 1900-2200. No smoking. Map 5, F2, p254* This neighbourhood restaurant is a little out of the way but well worth seeking out for its excellent fish and seafood. Not the most salubrious of interiors but that's not why people come here.

£ **Susie's Diner**, 51-53 West Nicolson St, **T** 667 8729. *Tue-Sat 0900-2100, Mon till 2000, Sun 1200-1900. Map 5, D4, p254* Self-service vegetarian/vegan diner offering a broad range of dishes, including Mediterranean and Middle Eastern. Popular with students and lecturers from the nearby University. Basic setting but always a nice vibe.

Cafés, sandwich bars and delis

The Engine Shed Café, 19 St Leonard's La, **T** 662 0040. *Mon-Thu 1030-1530, Fri till 1430, Sat till 1600, Sun 1100-1600. No smoking.*

Map 5, D6, p254 Tucked away in a residential area off St Leonard's St, this little vegetarian café provides just about the best-value lunch in town. Bread is baked on the premises and can be bought separately. Bakery and café provides work experience for adults with learning difficulties.

Kaffe Politik, 146-148 Marchmont Rd, **T** 446 9873. *Daily 1000-2100. Map 5, H2, p254* Stylish surroundings, healthy, vegetable-based food, excellent home-baking and good coffee. At its best on a lazy Sunday, enjoying brunch with the broadsheets.

Leith, Newhaven and Portobello

Restaurants, bistros, bars and brasseries

£££ (fitz)Henry, 19 Shore Pl, **T** 555 6625. *Mon-Fri 1200-1430, 1830-2230, Sat 1830-2230. Map 6, C7, p256* This stylish warehouse brasserie is incongruously located close to some seedy looking tenements but don't be put off. It has received awards for its genuinely original and excellent Scottish cooking and is up there with the city's finest.

£££ Restaurant Martin Wishart, 54 The Shore, **T** 553 3557. *Tue-Fri 1200-1400, 1900-2200; Sat 1900-2200. Map 6, C8, p256* Multi award-winning restaurant serving French-influenced cuisine at its very finest. A meal here is a truly memorable experience, as you'd expect from such a renowned chef as Martin Wishart, the only one in the city to receive a coveted Michelin star. The set two- and three-course lunches (£14.50 and £16.50 respectively) allow less fortunate souls to sample the delights on offer.

£££ Skippers, 1a Dock Pl, **T** 554 1018. *Mon-Sat 1230-1400, 1900-2200. Map 6, B7, p256* This nautical bistro is small and intimate, and very popular, so you'll need to book. Many in the know would say this is the best place to eat seafood in town.

£££ The Vintners Rooms, 87 Giles St, **T** 554 6767. *Mon-Sat 1200-1400, 1900-2230. Map 6, D7, p256* These former wine vaults dating from the 17th century now house a restaurant and bar, both lit by candlelight and oozing historic charm and romance. The food is French provincial and excellent, as is the service. Meals in the bar at lunchtime are cheaper.

££ Britannia Spice, 150 Commercial St, Britannia Way, **T** 555 2255. *Daily 1200-1415, 1700-2345. Map 6, B5, p256* Not a royal recruit to girl power but a welcome addition to Edinburgh's Asian cuisine scene, offering a tastebud-tingling combination of Bangladeshi, Nepalese, Thai, Sri Lankan and North Indian cooking.

££ Daniel's Bistro, 88 Commercial St, **T** 553 5933. *Daily 1000-2200. Map 6, B7, p256* Classic French food with an Alsace influence at unbeatable prices. Set lunch is ludicrously cheap at under £7 for three courses. Friendly atmosphere and always busy.

££ Fishers, 1 The Shore, **T** 554 5666. *Daily 1200-2230. Map 6, B8, p256* Housed in the tower at the end of The Shore, this is one of the city's finest fish restaurants, in an area packed full of them.

££ The Rock, 78 Commercial St, **T** 555 2225. *Tue-Fri 1200-1400, 1800-2200, Sat 1100-1600, 1800-2200, Sun 1100-1600. Map 6, B7, p256* One of many restaurants around here, this stands out from the rest for its sheer quality. The charcoal-grilled steaks are a major attraction but there's a much wider à la carte menu.

££ The Shore, 3-4 The Shore, **T** 553 5080. *Mon-Sat 1200-1430, 1830-2200, Sun 1230-1500, 1830-2200. No smoking. Map 6, C8, p256* Another of the city's best fish restaurants, this one is a cosy affair with a real fire and huge windows overlooking the Water of Leith. You can eat from the restaurant menu in the adjoining bar.

££ Tinelli, 139 Easter Rd, **T** 652 1932. *Tue-Sat 1200-1430, 1830-2300. Map 1, p247* This out-of-the-way Italian is one of the city's lesser-known stars but well worth the effort of finding it. Genuine Italian cooking of the highest quality and fantastic value. It's small and gets busy so book ahead.

££ The Waterfront, 1c Dock Pl, **T** 554 7427. *Mon-Thu 1200-2130, Fri/Sat 1200-2200, Sun 1230-2130. Bar Mon-Sat 1200-2400, Sun till 2300. Map 6, B7, p256* Great for fish or just for a relaxing drink, seated in the conservatory or outside on a sunny day.

££ Zinc Bar & Grill, Ocean Terminal, Victoria Dock, Leith, **T** 553 8070. *Sun-Thu 1200-2200, Fri/Sat 1200-2300. Map 6, A6, p256* Terence Conran's much-hyped entrance to the Edinburgh culinary scene has so far failed to excite or impress. Perhaps it's the rather cold and clinical surroundings, or slightly pretentious attitude, but no one can fail to be impressed by the view of Britannia moored on the other side of the vast window. On the food front, it's pukka bistro fare and though a bit pricey the prix fixe at £12 for two courses and £15 for three (served Monday-Friday 1200-1900) is a good bet.

West of the city

££ Marynka, 57 High St, Linlithgow, **T** 01506-840123. *Tue-Sat 1200-1400, 1800-2130.* Colourful little restaurant offering an eclectic range of very fine dishes. Worth stopping for if you've been to visit the palace.

East of the city

£££ La Pontiniere, Gullane main st, **T** 01620-843214. *Lunch Tue-Sat, dinner Fri and Sat only.* The best place to eat in the area is this French bistro. Its massive popularity means it's booked up well in advance.

££ Drover's Inn, East Linton, **T** 01620-860298. A great place for a pub lunch. You can sit outside on a sunny day, or stay inside in the cosy bistro. Either way, the food is excellent and worth the trip alone.

££ The Waterside Restaurant & Bistro, 1/5 Nungate, Haddington, **T** 01620-825764. *Mon-Fri 1130-1400, 1830-2200, Sat 1130-2200, Sun 1230-2100.* Excellent French bistro-style food downstairs and upstairs in the more expensive restaurant.

Edinburgh has more pubs and bars per square mile than any other European city. That may just be the drink talking, but the city does boast an inordinate amount of watering holes, from centuries-old pubs to the latest in contemporary urban chic. There's a bar for everyone in this town and, if that weren't enough, the city is blessed with the most liberal licensing laws in the UK. It is not a problem finding bars open till past midnight any night of the week and many are open till 0100 at weekends, and till 0300 during the Festival and the Christmas/New Year period. There are also bars on Leith Walk that open at 0500, in time for post clubbers still up for a good time. Festival Edinburgh is a place where you can party for 24 hours – as the saying goes: "You can sleep in September". The city's clubs, meanwhile, are no longer simply places to get a late drink. The club scene has undergone a dramatic transformation and any self-respecting raver will be well sorted for the latest dancefloor tunes spun by some of the UK's top DJs.

Edinburgh's most famous drinking street is Rose Street, a narrow pedestrianized lane between Princes Street and George Street, but it has seen better days and only one or two of its many hostelries are worthy of note. The prime drinking venue now is George Street and the streets running north and south of it. Here you'll find most of the city's hip and happening places. Another good destination is the area at the top of Leith Walk known as the "Pink Triangle", where there are many gay or gay-friendly cafés, bars and restaurants. The dark, narrow streets between the Chambers Street and the Royal Mile hide some good bars, especially the Cowgate, which joins the wide expanse of the Grassmarket, a big drinking street that gets very lively at weekends and is particularly popular with students and visiting hen and stag parties. An area with a diverse mix of drinking holes is Leith. Here you'll find everything from the roughest spit-and-sawdust joints to the trendiest waterside warehouse conversions. The city's club scene has now pretty much recovered from the effects of the fire that destroyed several venues at the end of 2002, with most nights finding new permanent homes.

Opening hours Note that in Scotland people tend to speak of bars rather than pubs and many of them listed here are open from 1100-0100 Monday-Saturday and 1230-2400 on Sunday. All of clubs venues listed open from between 2200-2230 to 0300 (Festival and Christmas/New Year also applies allowing opening to 0500). Standard charges are from £8-£10 for members and £10-£13 for non members.

Old Town

Bars

Beluga Bar, 30a Chambers St, **T** 624 4545. *Daily till 0100. Map 2, G5, p248* Vast basement drinking den housed in the former dental school and now regularly rammed with the city's toothsome twenty-somethings. Stylish décor and furnishings but not painfully hip (or not as much as it likes to think). The clientele are more interested in getting trousered than admiring each others' gear. Food in the ground floor bistro is fairly predictable and a tad pricey. DJs at weekends and live jazz on Sunday.

Bar Kohl, 54 George IV Bridge, **T** 225 6936. *Mon-Sat till 0100. Map 2, G4, p248* Recently extended and very busy bar which trades on the divergent themes of flavoured vodka and gangsta rap. The bar has over 50 different flavoured vodkas and a mixed clientele of clubbers, drinkers and Ali-G types (due to the constant hip-hop played on the stereo).

The Bow Bar, 80 West Bow, Victoria St, **T** 226 7667. *Mon-Sat till 2330, Sun till 2300. Map 2, G3, p248* No-nonsense, no frills pub for real ale enthusiasts and those who long for the days before mobile phones and sun-dried tomatoes. A dependable pint in an ever-changing world.

The Beehive Inn, 18-20 Grassmarket, **T** 225 7171. *Sun-Tue till 2400, Wed-Sat till 0100. Map 2, H2, p248*. Typically rowdy Grassmarket pub downstairs, but the restaurant upstairs is surprisingly intimate and serves good Scottish fare. Starting point for Literary Edinburgh tours (see p26).

City Café, 19 Blair St, **T** 220 0125. *Daily till 0100. Map 2, F6, p248* The daddy of Edinburgh's style bars and still the busiest and most vibrant pre-club venue in town. Done out like an American diner with chrome-topped bar and booth seating. Humungous platefuls of food served all day (chilli, burgers, etc) and a couple of pool tables. Set on two floors with a large bar area with pool tables to the rear on the top (ground) floor and smaller bar downstairs where funky House/Garage DJs play at weekends.

EH1, 197 High St, **T** 220 5277. *Daily 0930-0100.   Map 2, E6, p248* Slap bang in the heart of it all and close to the main clubs around the Cowgate/Royal Mile area. Outside seating, so great for people-watching, plus comfortable and stylish interior. Relaxed atmosphere is conducive to a lazy late breakfast. Small area at the back where DJs play on weekends for a distinctly up-for-it crowd of pre-clubbers.

Iguana, 41 Lothian St, **T** 220 4288. *Daily till 0100.   Map 2, H5, p248* This fashionable café-bar/bistro attracts students by day and pre-club ravers by night. Smart décor and DJs Friday/Saturday night. Large video screens. Very buzzy but it can be too noisy to maintain any form of conversation.

Negociants, 45-47 Lothian St, **T** 225 6313. *Daily till 0300.   Map 2, H5, p248* Great for a relaxing lunch-time beer or coffee, and popular with students and professionals alike. At night it's a fave late-night watering hole, with DJs and dancing downstairs, and a lifesaver for those poor souls suffering the midnight munchies. The menu is international in flavour, excellent value and available till way past your bedtime. Good place for a relaxing Sunday brunch to work off that hangover, and lots of outside seating in summer.

Oxygen Bar & Grill, 2-5 Infirmary St, **T** 557 9997. *Daily till 0100.   Map 2, G7, p249* A supremely cool and stylish place to eat or drink. Nice place to chill out with a beer or a coffee and fairly buzzes at weekends.

The Royal Oak, 1 Infirmary St. *Daily till 0200.   Map 2, G7, p249* If it's a late-night session of traditional folk music you're after, then look no further. Every night around 2200 there's a spontaneous outbreak of singing and fiddle playing, washed down with copious quantities of whisky and beer.

The Three Sisters, 139 Cowgate, **T** 622 6800. *Daily till 0100.* *Map 2, G5, p248* Fast becoming one of the city's liveliest venues. Huge, cavernous affair, divided into three sections: American bar at the entrance, leading into Irish theme bar and finally a Gothic-style bar at the far end. Huge courtyard out front gets very busy in summer and there's dancing nightly upstairs.

Clubs

The Bongo Club, 14 New St, **T** 556 5204. *Map 2, D8, p249* Cabaret-style venue for a wide variety of performing artists, aimed very much at the arty, bohemian crowd. Innovative, eccentric and pretentious in equal measure. Music nights include funky break-beat, trip hop and Latin. Operates a full and varied list of live acts every evening Monday-Thursday.

Cabaret Voltaire, 36 Blair St. *Map 2, F6, p248* Formerly home of The Honeycomb and Peppermint Lounge. Now refurbished and aiming to host a variety of performance art and avant garde acts during the week with club nights at weekends. The funky house *Ultragroove* has relocated from the burnt-out La Belle Angèle and runs fortnightly Saturdays.

Massa, 36-39 Market St. *Map 2, E5, p248* There are two sides to this venue, on a Friday from 1700 onwards its *TFI Friday* night is the most popular post-work venue for the city's office workers, and half price drinks are served till 2000 to a backdrop of Wham, Abba, young secretaries and leering bosses – not for the faint hearted. It also hosts *Eye Candy* and *Tackno* (see Gay and lesbian, p215).

The Honeycomb, 15 Niddry St. *Map 2, F7, p249* Formerly known as The Vaults some £100 million has been spent on its refurbishment. It was set to be sold early this year until most of its surrounding opposition was destroyed in the great fire of

December. Hosts on alternative Saturdays *Audio Deluxe* and *Do This Do That* (the latter night which often sees big name DJs visiting Edinburgh once again). The long-running Friday drum'n' bass night, *Manga*, has relocated from the fire-ravaged La Belle Angèle.

The Liquid Room, 9c Victoria St (top end), **T** 225 2564. *Map 2, G3, p248 See also p191* Now a very popular venue. Attracting many acts for gigs Monday-Thursday (particularly old punk acts) and hosting some of the city's biggest club nights at the weekends. Saturdays rotate between the long-running gay-friendly night *Luvely*, 70's cheese *Rewind*, live acts and *Colours* (which attracts many big name DJs). Sundays host the popular gay-friendly night *Taste*.

New Town

Bars

The Abbotsford, 3 Rose St, **T** 225 5276. *Mon-Sat till 2300. Map 2, C3, p248* Big, old reliable pub in a street that's largely lost its drinking appeal. Good, solid pub lunches and a restaurant upstairs open in the evenings.

Bar 38, 126-128 George St, **T** 220 6180. *Mon-Sat till 0100, Sun till 2400. Map 4, A12, p253* Large, spacious, contemporary bar with lots of chrome and blond wood. Popular with the after-work, young professional crowd.

Café Royal Circle Bar, 19 West Register St, **T** 556 4124. *Mon-Wed 1100-2300, Thu till 2400, Fri and Sat till 0100, Sun till 2300. Map 2, C4, p248* You can't help feeling spoiled in these elegant and civilized surroundings. Adjacent to the famous Café Royal Oyster Bar (see p151). Treat yourself to the seafood menu while enjoying the sumptuous splendour. Next door upstairs is the Café Royal Bistro Bar, a big favourite with the rugger fraternity.

Candy Bar, 113-115 George St, **T** 225 9179. *Daily till 0100. Map 4, A11, p253* Cosy and classy subterranean bar with a warm, unpretentious feel and good cocktail list. Simple, clean lines and an attractive design make it easy on the eye.

The Cumberland Bar, 1 Cumberland St, **T** 558 3134. *Mon-Wed till 2330, Thu-Sat till 2400, Sun till 2200. Map 3, F6, p250* Classic New Town bar that oozes refinement and respectability. Fine selection of real ales, a beer garden and some decent nosh. A good place to kick back and while away an hour or four.

The Guildford Arms, 1 West Register St. *Sun-Wed till 2300, Thu-Sat till 2400. Map 2, C5, p248* Ornate Victorian bar with an excellent selection of good ales.

Opal Lounge, 51a George St, **T** 226 2275. *Mon-Sat 1200-0300, Sun 1230-0300. Map 2, C1, p248* A night out in the capital doesn't get more fashionable than this. Cavernous subterranean bar and bistro with three other bar areas, sunken lounges for dining and dancing and plenty of sexy little nooks and crannies. Comfortable and relaxed vibe despite the high pose quotient, created by the sultry lighting, dark wood decor and chocolate furnishings. The menu is overwhelmingly Oriental in flavour and decent value.

YO! Below, underneath YO! Sushi (see p). *Daily till 0100. Map 2, C1, p248* A strange hybrid of Japanese entertainment with the offer of a post-sashimi head massage or tarot reading from the waitresses who also belt out the latest karaoke favourites and take requests. Beer comes from your own private tap and manga cartoons are shown on one wall. Alternatively, kick off your shoes and enjoy an intimate bottle of wine á deux on their giant beds.

Calton Hill and Broughton

Bars

Barony Bar, 81-85 Broughton St, **T** 557 0546. *Daily till 2400, Fri and Sat till 0030, Sun till 2300. Map 3, G9, p251* Stylish and lively place where you won't feel like you've gatecrashed your young nephew's party. Very busy at weekends. Good bar food.

Baroque, 39-41 Broughton St, **T** 557 0627. *Daily till 0100. Map 3, G9, p251* Brightly coloured décor that's not quite as loud as the young party-lovers who frequent this popular bar. Usual range of trendy pub grub and a great selection of juices.

The Basement, 10-12a Broughton St, **T** 557 0097. *Daily till 0100. Map 3, G9, p251* This Broughton Street original feels like it's always been around and is just as hip and happening as ever. Good bistro food with a mainly Mexican flavour, it's still one of the best-value meals in town.

Cask and Barrel, 115 Broughton St, **T** 556 3132. *Map 3, F9, p251* Set in the increasingly hip Broughton Street part of the New Town, but very different from many of the other, more glamorous places. Real Ale, brass taps and wooden fittings.

Mathers, 25 Broughton St, **T** 556 6754. *Mon-Thu till 2400, Fri and Sat till 0030, Sun till 2300. Map 3, G9, p251* A welcome respite from the unremitting cool of this part of the city. Just a plain and simple bar serving good beer and outrageously cheap food (fish and chips are £1.99) in relaxed surroundings.

The Outhouse, 12a Broughton St La, **T** 557 6668. *Daily till 0100. Map 3, G9, p251* Under the same management as Ego night

★ Best

Weird and wonderful interiors

- The Pond, p184
- The Vintners Rooms, 166
- Café Royal Oyster Bar, p151
- The Witchery by the Castle, p143
- The Canny Man's, p182

club, this small dark bar is not very plush but does fill up quickly and has a good atmosphere. A firm fave with pre-clubbers. Good beer garden in the summer months.

Pivo Caffé, 2-6 Calton Rd, **T** 557 2925. *Daily till 0100. Map 2, B6, p248* Czech-themed bar offering a thick slice of Prague, with pictures of the old city adorning the walls. As you'd expect, the lager is very good and the food, which is served in giant portions, is also worth Czech-ing out. Attracts a lot of students on their way to The Venue nightclub nearby so there's a buzz about the place later in the evening.

Pop Rokit, 2A Picardy Pl. *Map 3, G9, p251* Formerly The Catwalk, this cool little bar spread over two floors is mostly frequented by clubbers going to Ego and The Venue. Can be very quiet after 2200 at weekends.

Clubs

Ego, 14 Picardy Pl. *Map 3, G9, p251 See also Gay and lesbian p215* Refurbished casino hosting various well-established club nights, its biggest draws are *Vegas* which runs monthly and is frequented by twenty to thirty somethings who enjoy spending their Saturday nights dancing to Kenny Rogers, Neil Diamond and Johnny Cash; the 70's disco themed *Disco Inferno*; the long-running gay night *Joy* and its new sister club *Wiggle*. Fridays tend to host new clubs in the smaller Cocteau Lounge. Club nights in the summer months sometimes utilize the Outhouse's beer garden.

Studio 24, 24-26 Calton Rd. *Map 2, C10, p249* At opposite end of the street to The Venue. Dilapidated but nevertheless has good atmosphere. Hosts mainly grunge/rock nights for the city's young baggy-trousered, skateboard-wielding rock kids, including the long-running *Mission*. Splits into two separate venues (upstairs and downstairs) on fortnightly Saturdays for *Mingin* (see p215) while the Limp Bizkit fans retain the main room.

The Venue, 17-23 Calton Rd (behind Waverley Station), **T** 557 3073. *Map 2, C6, p248* Recently refurbished and under new management, Venue now hosts a variety of new up and coming soul, hip hop and house nights with a variety of live acts on week nights.

Stockbridge and Inverleith

Bars

The Antiquary, 72-78 St Stephen St, **T** 225 2858. *Mon-Wed till 0030, Thu-Sat till 0100, Sun till 2400. Map 3, G5, p250* The 'tick', as it's better known, is something of a local institution. Students come to this basement bar for the cheap food. On Fridays between 1700 and 1900 sandwiches and filled rolls are free.

The Baillie Bar, 2 St Stephen St, **T** 225 4673. *Map 3, G5, p250* Dark, smoky basement bar in Stockbridge. Attracts a more mature clientele and serves above-average food.

Hectors, 47-49 Deanhaugh St, **T** 343 1735. *Sun-Wed till 2400, Thu-Sat till 0100. Map 3, F4, p256* The place for bright young things to hang out in Stockbridge. Chill out with a glass of chilled Chardonnay, or do as the locals do and spend a lazy Sunday afternoon with the papers and a big brunch.

West Edinburgh

Bars

Bert's Bar, 29-31 William St, **T** 225 5748. *Mon-Wed till 2300, Thu-Sat till 2400. Map 4, B9, p253* A better class of rugby bar which attracts the more refined aficionado as well as the occasional Charlotte Street mafiosi. A pie and a pint doesn't get much better than this.

The Caley Sample Room, 58 Angle Park Terr, **T** 337 1006. *Map 4, F6, p252* Sells the full range of ales from the nearby Caledonian Brewery. Popular with rugby and footie fans enjoying a pre- or post-match pint with their pie and chips.

Cramond Inn, 30 Cramond Glebe Rd, Cramond Village, **T** 336 2035. *Mon-Fri 1200-1430, 1800-2130, Sat 1200-2130, Sun 1230-2130. Map 1, p247* Bucolic bliss only four miles from the city centre. Good selection of fresh fish and seafood, and good ales to wash it down. Outdoor seating in summer with views across the Forth.

Filmhouse Café Bar, 88 Lothian Rd, **T** 229 5932. *Sun-Thu till 2330, Fri/Sat till 0030. Map 4, C11, p253* Comfortable place to relax whether or not you're catching a movie. Busy at lunchtimes and evenings with a wide mix of people who come for coffee and chat or to enjoy the excellent-value vegetarian food.

Indigo Yard, 7 Charlotte La, **T** 220 5603. *Mon-Sat 1100-0100, Sun 1230-0100. Map 4, A10, p253* This converted and covered courtyard has been transformed into an immensely popular bar and restaurant. The menu is cosmopolitan (Thai, Mexican, French, Italian etc) and the food excellent. It has a good cocktail list and popular with weekend pre-clubbers. One of the places to be seen drinking in.

Mather's, 1 Queensferry St. *Mon-Thu till 2400, Fri and Sat till 0100. Map 4, B10, p253* This is a good real ale pub with a gorgeous interior.

Mondobbo, 34 Bread St, **T** 221 5555. *Mon-Thu and Sun till 2400, Fri and Sat till 0100. Map 4, C11, p253* Part of the supremely stylish Point Hotel, and don't it show. Popular with local office workers for a sophisticated light lunch or after work for happy-hour cocktails.

Traverse Bar Café, Traverse Theatre, 10 Cambridge St, **T** 228 5383. *Mon till 2300, Tue-Thu and Sun till 2400, Fri/Sat till 0100. Map 4, C11, p253* Very stylish bar that's popular with luvvies, suits and students. Excellent and affordable food served at all times, and regular special drinks offers.

Uluru, 133 Lothian Rd, **T** 228 5407. *Mon-Thu till 2400, Fri and Sat till 0100, Sun 1600-2400. Map 4, D11, p253* Relaxed, laid-back bar with an Aussie theme. Good place to chill during the day but gets busy at weekends. Cheap lunch specials and good range of cocktails if you're on the razz.

Clubs

The Ark, Semple St, **T** 229 7733. *Map 4, D11, p253*
Student-friendly venue where cheap drinks promotions and cheesy chart tunes rule the roost.

Cavendish/Diva, 3 West Tollcross, **T** 228 3252. *Map 4, D11, p253* Probably past its sell-by date as a major dance venue, but hosts The Mambo Club upstairs on weekends, playing African/reggae/Latin rhythms for a mixed crowd.

The Citrus Club, Grindlay St, **T** 662 7086. *Thu-Sun. Map 4, C11, p253* Mostly caters for the city's indie kids, though Sunday is devoted to 60s ska and northern soul. Also attracting gigs from old 70s/80s punk/ska bands.

The Subway West End, 23 Lothian Rd, **T** 229 9197. *Daily till 0300. Map 4, B11, p253* Real student haunt playing a wide mix including indie, 70s cheese and more mainstream dance.

South Edinburgh

Bars

Bennet's Bar, 8 Leven St, **T** 229 5143. *Mon-Wed till 2330, Thu-Sat till 0030, Sun till 2300. Map 4, E11, p253* Next to the King's Theatre. Marvel at the carved wooden gantry, the stained-glass windows, the huge mirrors, and the glass-topped tables with inlaid city maps while you enjoy a great pint of beer and perhaps some good old-fashioned (and cheap) food (served in the back room at lunchtime only). One of the city's finest traditional pubs.

The Canny Man's, 237 Morningside Rd. *Mon-Sat till 2400, Sun till 2300. Map 1, p247* Part museum/part pub that's been serving good real ale and a vast smorgasbord of sandwiches in most interesting surroundings since Victoria was on the throne, and probably to the same bunch of regulars.

Human Be-in, 2-8 West Crosscauseway, **T** 662 8860. *Daily till 0100. Map 5, D4, p254* Bein' so close to the Uni it gets its fair share of lecture dodgers who tend to hog the comfy booths, but if you can claim one it's worth staying to sample the tasty snacks or more substantial meals and enjoy the relaxed ambience.

The Pear Tree House, 38 West Nicolson St, **T** 667 7533. *Mon-Wed and Sun till 2400, Thu-Sat till 0100. Map 5, D4, p254* Near the University, so a favourite student haunt, this was once a focal point for the city's crusties but now the occasional suit can be spotted. Boasts Edinburgh's only decent-sized beer garden, which is not only packed in summer, but also populated at other times of the year. Also serves amazingly cheap food.

Leith, Newhaven and Portobello

Bars

Bar Java, 48-50 Constitution St, **T** 467 7527. *Mon-Wed 0700-2400, Thu and Fri till 0100, Sat and Sun 0800-2400. Map 6, C8, p256* Groovy little bar that opens early for breakfast, has a beer garden for those rare warm summer evenings, good food, live music and even rooms for B&B upstairs (see p138).

iso-bar, 7 Bernard St, **T** 467 8904. *Daily till 0100. Map 6, C8, p256* Looks like a mini IKEA from the outside but inside it's actually quite comfy, friendly and the food is good value.

King's Wark, 36 The Shore, **T** 554 9260. *Mon-Thu till 2300, Fri and Sat till 2400, Sun till 2300. Map 6, C8, p256* One of the oldest pubs in Leith, dating back to the early 17th century, and it appears not to have changed much. Real historical atmosphere and some excellent food (mid-range).

Old Salt, 17 Albert Pl, Leith Walk. Right on the border between Edinburgh and Leith, this old boozer opens at 0500 for postal workers, but at weekends is a curious mix of loved-up clubbers winding down and posties gearing up for the day's delivery.

The Pond, 2 Bath Rd, **T** 467 3825. *Mon-Thu 1600-0100, Fri-Sun 1400-0100. Map 6, C9, p256* Make no mistake, this place looks weird, but makes for an interesting drinking experience, and also effortlessly laid-back. Bit out of the way through an insalubrious part of Leith, but worth it.

You could be forgiven for thinking that once the Festival had packed its bags and gone, Edinburgh would be so exhausted that it would go into cultural hibernation, to appear refreshed and ready for the next one. Not a bit of it. True, the city's legendary festivals represent the single greatest arts extravaganza anywhere on the planet, but Edinburgh's citizens are up for a bit of cultural entertainment at any time. Instead of lying dormant for 48 weeks of the year, the theatres and concert halls play host to a vast range of local and touring productions – everything from Bach to Berkoff – and even the hungriest movie buff could not fail to be sated by the city's cinematic fare on offer at its wonderful little arthouse film theatres. Edinburgh is also the dance capital of Scotland, with the completion of Dancebase, the new multi-million pound National Centre for Dance.

Cinema

One of Edinburgh's most famous sons is the actor – and former city milkman – Sean Connery. Not surprising then that the city is also a popular location in which to shoot films. Many of these have been stories that are set in the city like *The Prime of Miss Jean Brodie*, *Shallow Grave*, *Complicity* and *Trainspotting*. But Edinburgh's ancient streets are so well preserved that it also serves as a useful 'double' for other British cities, when authentic period locations are required. It became Victorian England when the BBC shot *Great Expectations* here while *Jude*, the film version of Thomas Hardy's *Jude the Obscure* was also filmed in the city – Edinburgh this time acting as stand in for Cambridge.

The movie-going scene is dominated by the International film Festival, held at the legendary Filmhouse, which also hosts a number of foreign film seasons, most notably French (in November), Italian (in April) and a gay film season (in June). The city's other arthouse theatres are equally fecund, while the growth of multi-screen behemoths means that you're never far away from the latest Hollywood blockbuster.

The Cameo, 38 Home St, Tollcross, **T** 228 4141. *Map 4, E11, p253* Three screens showing new arthouse releases and cult classics (it premiered both *Pulp Fiction* and *Trainspotting*). Late showings at weekends and a good bar with comfy seating and snacks and video screen showing short films. Great place for movie buffs to hang out. The bar is open Sunday-Wednesday 1230-2300, Thursday-Saturday till 0100, and you can also enjoy a drink while watching a movie.

The Dominion, 18 Newbattle Terr, **T** 447 4771. *Map 4, H10, p253* A nice old-fashioned cinema down in Morningside. Three screens showing new releases.

Filmhouse, 88 Lothian Rd, **T** 228 2688. *Map 4, C11, p253* The UK's most famous regional cinema and the hub of Edinburgh's International Film Festival, so you never know who you might bump into. Three screens showing a wide range of movies, including new arthouse releases, obscure foreign films and old classics. The café-bar is a good place to hang out (see p180).

The Lumière, Royal Museum of Scotland, Chambers St, **T** 247 4219. *Map 2, H5, p248* At the rear of the museum. Runs a weekly programme Friday-Sunday with monthly themed seasons.

Odeon, 7 Clerk St, **T** 667 0971. *Map 5, E4, p254* Five-screen complex showing mainstream releases, plus the occasional arthouse/mainstream crossover.

Ster Century Cinemas, Ocean Terminal, **T** 553-0700, www.ster century.co.uk *Map 6, A6, p256* Luxurious 12-screen complex show ing all the latest releases.

Comedy

During the 80s alternative comedy was king and any aspiring comedian had to play the Edinburgh Festival if they wanted to make an impact. This is now less so, as more and more comedians preview their Edinburgh shows in London, but playing The Fringe is still de rigueur for any self-respecting funny person and the coveted Perrier Award, given to the brightest new comedy talent, remains the ultimate goal for all budding comedians. The legendary Gilded Balloon Theatre was tragically burned down in the terrible fire of December 2002, but it lives on in spirit at a series of alternative venues (listed on the next page). If you want to have your ribs tickled outside the Festival in Edinburgh, The Stand, has been joined by a branch of the famous comedy chain, Jongleurs.

Assembly Rooms and Music Hall, 54 George St, **T** 226 2428. *Map 2, C1, p248* One of the main Fringe venues, hosting a huge variety of mainly higher quality drama productions and more established comedians. It is also used throughout the year, though its future is uncertain at the time of writing.

Gilded Balloon, **T** 226 6550 (information), **T** 226 2151 (tickets), www.gildedballoon.co.uk The main venue is **Teviot**, 5/2 Bristo Sq. *Map 5, D3, p254* Comedy central, with six performance spaces in the University Student Union building. There's also **Caves I, II, and III**, South Niddry St, off Cowgate, *Map 2, G7, p249*, which is weird, spooky and subterranean; and **Peppermint Lounge**, 36 Blair St. *Map 2, F6, p248*

Jongleurs Comedy Club opens in the new Omni complex beside the Playhouse Theatre in July 2003. For details visit www.jongleurs.com *Map 2, A6, p248* Box office: **T** 0870-7870707.

Pleasance Theatre, 60 The Pleasance, **T** 556 6550. *Map 2, G9, p249* One of the top Fringe venues staging comedy and drama. The outdoor cobbled courtyard is a great place to hang out during the Festival for a bit of star-spotting.

The Stand Comedy Club, 5 York Pl, **T** 558 7272, www.thestand. co.uk *Mon-Thu 1200-2400, Fri 1200-1900, 1930-0100, Sat 1930-0100, Sun 1230-2400. £6.* *Map 2, A4, p248* This is the showcase for emerging comedy talent seven nights a week. By day it's a popular café-bar serving budget lunches, and on Sunday there's free comedy with your lunch. *OOT on Tuesday* is a monthly comedy night with gay and gay-friendly acts. Compered by the campest comedian in town, Scotland's very own Craig Hill. Runs on the second Tuesday of the month at 1930.

Dance

Edinburgh plays host to the world's top dance companies during the Festival but the arrival of the £6 mn lottery-funded national centre for dance in Scotland means that the capital attracts national and international dance companies throughout the year.

Dance Base, **T** 225 5525, www.dancebase.co.uk *Map 2, H2, p248* The facilities include four studios and the largest dance space available for public use in the UK. The building itself is a superb example of modern architecture and was on the short list for the RIBA's Stirling Prize. It utilizes the dramatic setting, below the precipitous slopes of Castle Rock, and is airy and spacious with high glass roofs to enhance the feeling of space.

Music

Glasgow may be the home of Scottish Opera and the National Symphony Orchestra but the capital's classical venues are by no means outclassed, offering a full and varied season. Edinburgh's indie music scene lacks the fecundity of its great rival, Glasgow, and beyond Finlay Quaye (remember him?), Shirley Mansun of Garbage and the Proclaimers, the city's contribution to the world of pop and rock is neglible. As befits the birthplace of the great saxophonist, Tommy Smith, its jazz scene is altogther healthier, and the city's enthusiastic folk performers can be seen 'geein' it laldy' on any given night of the week.

Classical

Usher Hall, Lothian Rd and Grindlay St, **T** 228 1155. *Map 4, C11, p253* The main civic concert hall and venue for frequent classical concerts by one of the national orchestras.

Queen's Hall, 89 Clerk St, **T** 668 2019.   *Map 5, E5, p254*   Smaller classical ensembles, as well as jazz, blues, folk, rock and pop.

Festival Theatre, Nicolson St, **T** 529 6000.   *Map 2, H7, p249* Excellent classical and opera venue with the occasional foray into pop. The glass-fronted café is a great place to sit and watch the world go by.

Reid Concert Hall, Bristo Sq, **T** 650 4367.   *Map 5, D3, p254* Stages less frequent performances.

St Cecilia's Hall, Cowgate and Niddry St, **T** 650 2805.   *Map 2, F7, p249. See also p54*   Wonderful 18th-century venue for occasional concerts.

Rock and pop

The Liquid Room (details on p175), has established itself as a good place to see touring acts such as Moby and Mogwai. They also host the T on the Fringe music festival.

The Attic, Cowgate, **T** 225 8382.   *Map 2, G5, p248*   Since the closure of the West Port's Cas Rock this has become the focal point for new talent in the capital. During The Fringe they host their own mini music festival called Planet Pop.

Royal Highland Exhibition Centre, Ingliston, **T** 333 2483. More ad hoc venue which is called into action when the stadium rock dinosaurs such as U2 and the Rolling Stones shuffle into town.

Edinburgh Playhouse (details under Theatre, p193) is a favourite with old codgers like Lou Reed and Van Morrison.

Corn Exchange, New Market Rd, Gorgie, **T** 443 2437.
Map 1, p247 Edinburgh's newest venue, the 3,000-capacity Corn Exchange, may lack atmosphere but at least offers an east coast alternative to Glasgow's Barrowlands.

Ross Open Air Theatre, Princes Street Gardens, **T** 220 4351.
Map 2, E1, p248 Has recently been used for major music gigs at Hogmanay and during the Festival.

Folk and country

The Royal Oak (see p173 for details) is one of the best places to hear authentic grassroots folk music in the city.

The Tron, 9 Hunter Sq, behind the Tron Kirk, **T** 220 1550. *Sun-Thu till 2400, Fri-Sat till 0100. Map 2, F6, p248* Below the ground floor bar are two basement levels, with regular folk sessions and a comedy club.

Whistlebinkies, Niddry St, **T** 557 5114. *Map 2, F6, p248*
Late-night venue where you can listen to some raucous folk or country till 0300.

West End Hotel, 35 Palmerston Pl, **T** 225 3656. *Map 4, B8, p253*
Popular with visiting Highlanders and also a good place to find out where and when ceilidhs are taking place in the city.

Jazz and blues

Henry's Cellar Bar, Morrison St, **T** 221 1228. *Map 4, C11, p253*
The best place to experience Edinburgh's vibrant jazz scene. This tiny cellar bar shows a vast-range of modern jazz acts, as well as hip hop, funk and soul. If you get there early, you can tuck into various Oriental culinary delights, as this is part of a trio of Chinese

restaurants. Nice! Occasional jazz concerts, as well as a growing number of top rock and pop gigs, also take place at the Queen's Hall (see p191). For details of the Jazz & Blues Festival, see p198.

Theatre

The theatre scene in Edinburgh reaches its peak during the Festival, when productions featuring everyone from established stars to hopeful students take place in a weird and wonderful variety of venues. The city operates at a frenetic pace that is impossible to sustain for any longer than a few weeks and things inevitably quieten down when the Festival and the Fringe are over. However, that doesn't mean that there isn't still plenty going on. You can see everything in Edinburgh from performances by international opera singers to plays by the hottest contemporary writers.

Bedlam Theatre, 11b Bristo Pl, **T** 225 9893, www.eusa.ed. ac.uk/societies/bedlam/ *Map 2, H4, p248* Lower key productions take place at this neo-gothic church, home of the university's Bedlam Theatre Company. Intellectual plays alternate with typically studenty improvised comedy shows.

Edinburgh Playhouse, 18-22 Greenside Pl, **T** 557 2590, www.edinburgh-playhouse.co.uk *Map 2, A7, p249* A huge barn of a theatre which can seat 3,000. The main venue for West End, Andrew Lloyd Webber-type musicals and the occasional ballet.

Festival Theatre, 13-29 Nicolson St, **T** 529 6000, www.eft.co.uk *Map 2, H7, p249* You might see anything here from Polish Opera performing La Bohème to the Scottish Ballet putting on a performance of *The Nutcracker*. It's a theatre that lends a sense of occasion to productions, and has the biggest stage in Scotland. Good coffee shop and a lively bar.

King's Theatre, 2 Leven St, **T** 529 6000, www.eft.co.uk
Map 4, E12, p253 Good, old-fashioned plays and pantos are performed here, often featuring TV stars in the cast.

Netherbow Centre, 43-45 High St, **T** 556 9579, www.storytelling centre.org.uk *Map 2, E7, p249* Specializes in children's shows and storytelling, and also stages community shows and amateur plays. Every year around November it hosts a Storytelling Festival.

Royal Lyceum Theatre, Grindlay St, **T** 248 4848, www.lyceum. org.uk *Map 4, C11, p253*   Stages its own quality productions of plays, pantos and musicals. You can see everything here from Shakespeare to *Cinderella*.

Theatre Workshop, 34 Hamilton Pl, **T** 226 5425 (box office), **T** 225 7942 (admin).   *Map 3, G4, p250* They stage four innovative productions each year including a community play, featuring local amateurs, and a hard-hitting issues-based production. They also run theatre workshops covering acting, stage management and marketing.

Traverse Theatre, Cambridge St, **T** 228 1404, www.traverse. co.uk *Map 4, C11, p253* The city's most exciting venue, a new writing theatre which commissions works from contemporary playwrights, not only from Scotland but throughout the world. Special events are held as well, such as the monthly Monday Lizard in which short scripts by tomorrow's writers are read by actors in the Traverse Bar. Both the bar and the bistro blue (see p160) are essential hang-out places during the Festival Fringe.

Every year Edinburgh plays host to the world's biggest arts festival, when the capital bursts into life in a riot of entertainment unmatched anywhere. Edinburgh during its Festival has been described as "the cultural hub of the world". Over a million tourists descend on the city to experience a brain-sapping variety of acts performed in a frightening variety of venues across the city. The Edinburgh Festival is actually a collection of different festivals running alongside each other, from the end of July through to the beginning of September. The big names in the International Festival need to booked up months in advance, and the growth of internet booking has also meant that many of the better-known Fringe acts are sold out well in advance. But it's still possible to leave it till you arrive in the city to draft an itinerary – especially if you're prepared to take a few risks. The city's other great celebrations are of more visceral than cerebral appeal, such as the pagan Beltane Festival and Hogmanay which has grown over the years to become the largest street party in the northern hemisphere.

April

Beltane (30) A wild party held on Calton Hill from 2200 till dawn, incorporates various ancient seasonal and fertility rites, including the passing of winter into spring.

Folk Festival Massive event at the beginning of April. Draws performers from near and far, **T** 554 3092.

Science Festival (11-22, 2003) Exhibitions, workshops, lectures and various hands-on events for adults and children alike. Box office: 21 Market Street, **T** 473 2070. *Map 2, E4, p248*

May

Scottish International Children's Festival (26 May-4 June, 2003) The UK's largest performing arts festival for children, held at the end of May. Box office: 45a George Street, **T** 225 8050, www.imaginate.org.uk *Map 2, C1, p248*

June

Royal Highland Show Held at the Royal Highland Centre, Ingliston, **T** 335 6200, at the end of June. It's a sort of display of the best of rural Scotland, with pedigree livestock competitions, flower shows, craft fairs and showjumping, amongst other things.

Caledonian Beer Festival Held at Edinburgh's own Caledonian Brewery on Slateford Road (see p93) around the first week of the month. The event features dozens of real ales, food and live music (mostly jazz) in the brewery's Festival Hall. See local press for details, or **T** 337 1286.

Pride, currently cancelled, but previously it has taken place every June when it alternates annually between Edinburgh and Glasgow. Check the notice boards at The Blue Moon Café (see p218).

July

International Jazz and Blues Festival (25 July-3 August, 2003) Kicks the whole thing off and features some of the world's leading performers, as well as many lesser-known ones, playing in just about every pub in the city centre and larger venues such as the Playhouse. There's also the free Jazz on a Summer's Day in Princes Street Gardens and Mardi Gras in the Grassmarket. Box office: 29 St Stephen St, **T** 667 7776 (information line **T** 467 5200), www.jazzmusic.co.uk *Map 3, G5, p250*

August

Edinburgh International Festival (10-30, 2003) The International Festival tends to be a fairly highbrow affair and features large-scale productions of opera, ballet, classical music, dance and theatre performed in the larger venues. It ends with an open air concert and spectacular fireworks display in Princes Street Gardens. Box office: The Hub, Castlehill, **T** 473 2000, www.eif.co.uk *Daily 0930-1730. Map 2, F3, p248* For details on all the events and to access the other festival websites visit www.edinburghfestivals.co.uk The free daily listings magazine, *The Guide*, is a good way to find out what's on and where. *The List* and *The Scotsman* also give comprehensive coverage.

The Fringe (3-25, 2003) A performing duck, a stuffed badger, genital origami and a lift in which a circus performer ties himself in knots for an audience of one. It can only mean one thing – the start of the Edinburgh Festival Fringe. Last year's Fringe saw over 500 companies performing in nearly 200 venues. So relax. You cannot

Fringe benefits

The Edinburgh Festival began life in 1947, conceived initially as an antidote to wartime austerity. In the early days it focused on music and theatre, under the guiding hand of its first director, the Austrian-born Sir Rudolph Bing, former manager of Glyndebourne, who left Edinburgh in 1949 to run the Metropolitan Opera House in New York. In its first year, the Festival saw such luminaries as Alec Guinness appear (in Shakespeare's *Richard II*), and the Film Festival was opened by John Grierson, the founding father of British documentary cinema. The following year, Edinburgh hosted the premiere of TS Eliot's *The Cocktail Party*. That same year, a local paper noted an enterprising development 'round the fringe of official drama'. This 'enterprising fringe' soon became known simply as The Fringe, and would go on to earn a reputation for pushing back the boundaries of art and entertainment. Over the years the Fringe has been a major showcase for fresh talent and the likes of Billy Connolly, Maggie Smith, Rowan Atkinson and Harry Enfield all started out here. Though criticised in the past few years for becoming too commercially-motivated and accused of being too big for its own good, The Fringe remains as innovative and experimental as ever and continues to be the launching pad for many of the UK's greatest actors, comedians, writers and directors.

possibly see everything, and you really wouldn't want to anyway. A good opportunity to preview many of the Fringe performers for free is Fringe Sunday, which takes place in Holyrood Park, at the foot of the Royal Mile. Box office: 108 High St, **T** 226-5257, www.edfringe.com *Daily 1000-1900 from mid-Jul till the end of the Festival. Map 2, E8, p249* Programme available in June.

International Book Festival (9-25, 2003) This may look like just a bunch of tents in Charlotte Square, but the marquees are full of some of the biggest names in literature holding readings, discussions, interviews and a whole range of workshops for adults and children. Box office: 137 Dundas St, **T** 228 5444, www.edbookfest.co.uk

Edinburgh International Film Festival (13-24, 2003) The UK's most important film festival with screenings of many brilliant new movies long before they reach London and the rest of the country. It is also the longest continually running event of its kind in the world and a great place to rub shoulders with some big names. Box office: Filmhouse, 88 Lothian Road, **T** 229 2550, www.edfilmfest.org.uk *Map 4, C11, p253*

Edinburgh Military Tattoo (1-23, 2003) Although it's a separate event, the Tattoo is very much part of the Festival, set against the magnificent backdrop of Edinburgh Castle. It's an unashamedly kilt-and-bagpipes event, featuring Massed Pipes and Drums, display teams, dancers and bands from all over the world. Box office: 32 Market Street, **T** 225 1188, www.edintattoo.co.uk *Mon-Fri 1000-1630; during the Festival Mon-Fri 1000-2100, Sat 1000-2230. Map 2, E4, p248*

December

Hogmanay (29 December-1 January) The millennium party was described as the best on earth and Edinburgh's New Year celebration continues to be one of the world's best festivals. It starts with a torchlit procession through the city centre followed by four days of various events, including pop and rock concerts. The highlight is the giant street party on the 31st (which is for ticket holders only). For information, **T** 473 3800, www.edinburghshogmanay.org

If shopping be your drug of choice then a trip to Edinburgh will produce a very satisfactory high. It's a city with shops to suit all tastes, from arriviste upstart Harvey Nicks to the well-bred Jenners, the city's answer to Harrods. Those in search of tartan tat should head for the Royal Mile which is lined with shops selling all manner of Caledonian kitsch: kilts, whisky, fluffy haggis, 'see you, Jimmy' hats and those scary tartan-clad dolls with flickering eyelashes. Any fashionista worth their low-sodium substitute should head straight for George Street which is wall-to-wall designer stores. Princes Street, once the city's main retail thoroughfare, is more downmarket and indistinguishable from too many other city centre streets (except for the views, of course). Good places to look for second-hand clothes and books, and antique art and jewellery are around the New Town and Stockbridge, Broughton Street and the Grassmarket. Victoria Street is worth a browse for something a bit different, while Cockburn Street is where you'll get your fix of sex, drugs and rock'n'roll.

Art and antiques

Blackadder Gallery, Raeburn Pl, **T** 332 4605. *Map 3, F3, p250*
Sells unusual gifts and prints.

Flux, 55 Bernard St, www.get-to-flux.co.uk *Map 6, C8, p256*
Proceeds go towards helping young artists.

Ingleby Gallery, 6 Carlton Terr, **T** 556 4441. *Map 2, A12, p249*
*Wed-Sat 1000-1700.*This selling gallery occupies the ground floor of
a Georgian house and includes work by Patrick Heron and Ian
Hamilton.

Just Junk, 34 Broughton St, **T** 557 6353. *Mon-Sat 1100-1800.*
Map 3, G9, p251 Small, reasonably priced range of stuff from the
50s and 60s.

Utilities, 87 Broughton St, **T** 557 4385. *Tue-Sat 1030-1830, Sun*
1200-1600. *Map 3, G9, p251* A real Aladdin's Cave where you
could lose hours just browsing.

Books

Armchair Books, 72 West Port, **T** 229 5927. *Map 4, C12, p253*
Everything a second-hand bookshop should be. Full to bursting
with some hidden gems.

Blackwell's, 53-59 South Bridge, **T** 556 6743. *Mon, Wed-Fri*
0900-2000, Tue 0930-2000, Sat 0900-1800, Sun 1100-1700. *Map 2,*
G7, p249 Formerly James Thin. The largest academic bookshop
in Scotland.

Broughton Books, 2a Broughton Pl, **T** 557 8010. *Map 3, F9,*
p251 Great place to browse for second-hand books and rarities.

Old Grindle's Bookshop, 3 Spittal St, **T** 229 7252. *Map 4, C11, p253* Small but good selection of second-hand books.

Ottakers, 57 George St, **T** 225 4495. *Mon, Wed, Fri 0900-1800, Tue 0930-1800, Thu 0900-2000, Sun 1130-1730. Map 2, C1, p248* Formerly James Thin. Good for kids' books and magazines.

Waterstone's, 128 Princes St, **T** 226 2666. *Mon-Sat 0830-2000, Sun 1030-1900. Map 4, A12, p253* Massive range of titles, well-informed staff and a pleasant second-floor café with fantastic views of the Castle. Other branches at: 13-14 Princes St, **T** 556 3034. *Map 2, C5, p248* ; and 83 George St, **T** 225 3436. *Map 2, C1, p248*

Clothes

Armstrongs, 83 Grassmarket, **T** 220 5557. *Map 2, G3, p248* Whether you're into retro clothing or simply dressing up for a theme night, this is where it's at.

Corniche, 14 Jeffrey St, **T** 556 3707. *Mon-Sat 1000-1730. Map 2, E8, p249* Stocks all the top names in women's fashion.

George Street is *the* place to come looking for more upmarket clothes shops. *Map 2, C1, p248* For the ladies there's: **Coast**, No 61, **T** 225 9190; **Escada**, No 35a, **T** 225 9885; **Jigsaw**, No 49, **T** 225 4501; **Karen Millen**, No 53, **T** 220 1589; **Phase Eight**, No 47b, **T** 226 4009; **The Cashmere Store**, No 67, **T** 226 4861. For gents there's: **Crombie**, No 63, **T** 226 1612; **Cruise**, No 94, **T** 226 3524; **Jigsaw Menswear**, No 103, **T** 226 7362; **Slater**, No 102, **T** 220 4343.

Shopping

Jane Davidson, 52 Thistle St, **T** 225 3280. *Map 2, B1, p248* Sells brands like Christian Dior.

Judith Glue, 64 High St, **T** 556 5443. *Mon-Sat 0930-1800, Sun 1200-1700. Map 2, E9, p249* Great for traditional knitwear.

McCalls of the Royal Mile, 11 High St, **T** 557 3979. *Map 2, E7, p249* A good place to get kilted out.

Pie in the Sky, 21 Cockburn St, **T** 220 1477. *Map 2, E5, p248* The ultimate hippy trip, man, with loon pants, bangles, baubles and beads and tons of tie-dyed stuff.

Schuh, 6 Frederick St, **T** 220 0290. *Map 2, D1, p248*; 32 North Bridge, **T** 225 6552 *Map 2, E6, p248* Everything from sparkly slingbacks to Doc Martens.

Smiths, 124 High St, **T** 225 5927. *Map 2, E6, p248* Top British designer menswear.

Department stores

Harvey Nichols, 30-34 St Andrew Sq, **T** 524 8388. *Map 2, B4, p248* Designer heaven. 90,000 sq ft of high fashion spread over five glorious floors. They're all here, from Stella McCartney to Alexander McQueen, via Gucci, Prada and Donna Karan.

Jenners, 48 Princes St, **T** 225 2442. *Mon and Wed 0900-1730; Tue 0930-1730; Thu 0900-1930; Fri and Sat 0900-1800. Map 2, C3, p248* Traditional department store selling everything from soft furnishings to designer clothes. The food hall is well worth a visit and is stuffed with traditional Scottish delicacies.

Food and drink

Ian Mellis, 30a Victoria St, **T** 226 6215. *Map 2, F3, p248*; 205 Bruntsfield Pl, **T** 447 8889. *Map 4, G10, p253*; North West Circus Pl, **T** 225 6566. *Map 3, G5, p250* Cheesemonger extraordinaire, where you can buy unusual cheeses like Gubbeen and Berkswell.

Lupe Pintos, 24 Leven St, **T** 228 6241. *Map 4, E11, p253* Delicioso Latin American and Spanish deli.

Peckhams, 155-159 Bruntsfield Pl, **T** 229 7054. *Map 4, G10, p253 Daily till 2200*. Fine vintners and victualers that will leave you salivating and quite a few quid lighter.

Royal Mile Whiskies, 379 High St, **T** 225 3383. *Map 2, F4, p248* Sells around 300 types of whisky.

Valvona & Crolla, 19 Elm Row. *Mon-Wed and Sat 0800-1800, Thu-Fri till 1930. Map 3, F10, p251 See also Cafés p158* Superb Italian deli importing fresh produce direct from Italy.

Villeneuve Wines, 49a Broughton St, **T** 558 8441. *Map 3, G9, p251* Great selection and knowledgeable staff.

Jewellery

Hamilton & Inches, 87 George St, **T** 225 4898. *Mon-Sat 0900-1800. Map 2, C1, p248* Upmarket jewellers' where the prices are such that, if you have to ask how much something is, you probably can't afford it.

Joseph Bonnar, 72 Thistle St, **T** 226 2811. *Map 3, H6, p250* Stocks a good range of fine quality antique jewellery.

Montresor, 35 St Stephen St, **T** 220 6877. *Map 3, G5, p250*
Sells fabulous antique and costume jewellery.

Music

Fopp, 55 Cockburn St, **T** 220 0133. *Map 2, E5, p248* Popular high
street chain with lots of good deals.

MMM, at The Hub, Castlehill, **T** 225 7601. *Map 2, F3, p248*
For something a wee bit more traditional and folky.

Blackfriar's Folk Music Shop, 49 Blackfriar's St (off the Royal
Mile), **T** 557 3090. *Map 2, F7, p249* Wide range of traditional
Scottish musical instruments.

Ripping Records, 91 South Bridge, **T** 226 7010. *Map 2, F6, p248*
Limited selection of mainstream CDs, but best known as the place
to buy tickets for any gig in the country.

Outdoor and leisure

Graham Tiso, 123 Rose St, **T** 225 9486. *Map 2, C1, p248* Excellent
for all kinds of outdoor clothing and sports equipment.

Shopping malls

Ocean Terminal, Ocean Dr, Leith, **T** 555 8888. *Mon-Fri 1000-
2000, Sat 0900-1900, Sun 1100-1800. Map 6, C1, p256* High Street
fashion outlets, bars, restaurants (see p167) and cinema (see p188).

Princes Mall, between the train station and Tourist Information
Centre. *Mon-Sat 0830-1800; Thu till 1900; Sun 1100-1700. Map 2,
C5, p248* There are a couple of good fashion outlets here, includ-
ing USC and Xile, as well as a number of eateries.

St James Centre, east end of Princes St. *Map 2, C5, p248* Houses all the usual High Street suspects as well as John Lewis, one of the city's major department stores.

Speciality

The Cigar Box, 361 High St, **T** 225 3534. *Map 2, F4, p248* This is Havana heaven for cigar-lovers.

Paper Tiger, 53 Lothian Rd, **T** 228 2790. *Map 4, C11, p253* Stylish and funky selection of greetings cards.

Robert Cresser, Victoria St, **T** 225 2181. *Map 2, F4, p248* Staff won't give you the brush-off in this traditional and much-photographed brush shop.

Whiplash Trash, 53 Cockburn St, **T** 226 1005. *Map 2, F3, p248* Haggis and whisky this ain't. Loads of cannabis paraphernalia and adult toys.

Those who need to escape even this most open of urban centres can rest easily in the knowledge that there are wild and rugged hills lying just beyond the southern limits. The Pentlands also offer horse riding and mountain biking opportunities and even a dry ski slope. Closer to home, Arthur's Seat is enough to get most people's pulses racing. Less active souls can don Pringle sweater and dodgy slacks and enjoy some of the best golf available anywhere along the stretch of East Lothian coast. Adrenaline junkies won't be disappointed either. Just to the west of the city is the brand new Adventure Centre, the most advanced and well-equipped rock climbing facility in the world. Edinburgh is the home of Scottish rugby. The national side play at Murrayfield Stadium in the west of the city and anyone with a penchant for major sporting events should try to find a ticket when Scotland play a Six Nations match or host a touring side from the southern hemisphere.

Football

Edinburgh has two Premier League teams, who play at home on alternate Saturdays during the league season. **Heart of Midlothian**, or Hearts, play at Tynecastle, on the Gorgie Road about a mile west of Haymarket, and **Hibernian** (Hibs) play at Easter Road, east of the centre near Leith. The domestic football season runs from early August to mid-May. Most matches are played on Saturdays at 1500, and there are often games through the week, on Tuesday and Wednesday evenings at 1930. There is usually a match on a Sunday afternoon, which is broadcast live on satellite TV. Tickets range from £15 up to £20-25 for big games.

Golf

There are many fine golf courses around Edinburgh, especially along the coast of East Lothian, but most are private. The best of these are at **Gullane** (Nos 1, 2 and 3), **T** 01620-842255, **Muirfield**, **T** 01620-842123, and **North Berwick**, **T** 01620, 895040. Prices for a weekday round range from £17 for Gullane No 3 up to £85 for Muirfield. Public courses in and around the city include the two at **Braid Hills**, **T** 447 6666, **Silverknowes**, **T** 336 3843, **Torphin Hill**, **T** 441 4061, and **Lothianburn**, **T** 445 2288. If you plan on playing a lot of golf, then you should buy the Lothian and Edinburgh Golf Pass, which allows you to play on 20 courses throughout the region at discounted rates. For details, contact the tourist board, **T** 473 3800, www.edinburgh.org/golf

Health and fitness

Escape, at the Scotsman Hotel (see p120), **T** 622 3800, www.escapehealthclubs.com State-of-the-art gym and fitness centre, beauty spa, sauna and 16-m stainless steel pool.

Meadowbank Sports Centre, 139 London Rd, **T** 661 5351. *Mon 0930-2300, Tue-Sun 0900-2300. To get there, take bus no 15 or 26 from Princes St (north side) or a no 45 from the Mound. Map 1, p247* The city's main venue for athletics meetings. Indoor and outdoor multi-sports complex with fitness room, squash courts, all-weather pitches, velodrome and climbing wall.

One Spa, 8 Conference Sq, **T** 221 7777, www.one-spa.com *Map 4, C10, p253* The ultimate in pampering, from a simple back massage (£38) to the full Ayurverdic Holistic Body Treatment (£110).

Horse racing

Musselburgh Racecourse, Linkfield Rd, Musselburgh, **T** 665 2859, www.musselburgh-racecourse.co.uk Stages 22 race meets per year. Admission: Club stand £12, Grandstand £7.

Horse riding

Edinburgh & Lasswade Riding Centre, Kevock Rd, Lasswade, **T** 663 7676. **Pentland Hills Icelandics**, Windy Gowl Farm, Carlops, near West Linton, **T** 01968-661095. **Tower Farm Riding Stables**, 85 Liberton Dr, **T** 664 3375.

Rock climbing

Adventure Centre, Ratho village, off A8, 10 mins west of Edinburgh airport, **T** 229 3919, www.adventurescotland.com An old quarry has been converted into a massive rock climbing and sports training venue. Home to the National Rock Climbing Centre, and the largest climbing arena in the world with 5,000 sq m of outdoor rock cliffs, 2,400 sq m of artificial wall and the only covered natural rock walls in the world. Includes AirPark, a suspended aerial adventure ropes ride, and an adventure sports gym. At the time of going to press a precise opneing date had not been confirmed, but it's expected to be around August 2003.

Rugby Union

The national team plays at Murrayfield and during match weekends there's always a great atmosphere in the city. Every year, in February and March, Scotland takes part in the Six Nations Championship. Tickets for games are hard to come by, but you can contact the Scottish Rugby Union (SRU), **T** 346 5000, for details of upcoming home fixtures and where to find tickets.

Scuba diving

Deep Blue Scuba, 1 Warriston Rd, **T/F** 556 2635, www.deepbluescuba   Also have a diving school at the Adventure Centre, see above.

Skiing

Midlothian Ski Centre, at Hillend (take the A702 off the City Bypass at the Lothianburn exit, or bus No 4 from the city centre), **T** 445 4433. *Mon-Sat 0930-2100, Sun 0930-1900.* Artificial ski slope for ski and snowboarding practice and instruction. Also downhill mountain bike trail and chairlift for those who want to admire the view.

Swimming

Ainslie Park Leisure Centre, 92 Pilton Dr, **T** 551 2400. *Mon-Fri 1000-2200, Sat-Sun 1000-1800. Take bus No 28 or 29 from the Mound to Crewe Toll, or 27 to Ferry Rd.* Swimming pool, sauna, steam room, spa, gym, fitness suite.

Leith Waterworld, 377 Easter Rd, **T** 555 6000. *Mon-Fri 0900-1700, Sat-Sun 1000-1700 during school holidays.* Good children's facilities.

Royal Commonwealth Pool, Dalkeith Rd, **T** 667 7211. *Mon-Fri 0900-2100, Sat-Sun 1000-1600. To get there take a No 14, 21, 33, 82 or 83 bus south from North Bridge.* *Map 5, F6, p254* The biggest and most popular in the city, with a 50-m pool, flumes, diving pool, children's area, sauna and gym.

Tennis

Craiglockart Tennis and Sports Centre, 177 Colinton Rd, **T** 443 0101. *Mon-Thu 0900-2300, Fri 1000-2300, Sat-Sun 0900-2230. Take bus No 10 from Princes St (south side) or No 27 from the Mound going south.* Indoor and outdoor tennis courts, squash, badminton, gym, fitness studio and free weights.

Walking

Geowalks, 23 Summerfield Place, **T** 555 5488, www.geowalks. demon.co.uk Guided walking tours of Arthur's Seat.

Leith Walks, 11 Madeira Place, **T** 555 2500, www.leithwalks. co.uk Walking tours around Edinburgh and the Pentland Hills.

Walkabout Scotland, **T** 661 7168, www.walkabout scotland.com Organize various day tours to the Highlands for some real hill-walking. All tours cost £40 per person (concessions £35). You'll need warm and waterproof clothing, good boots and water.

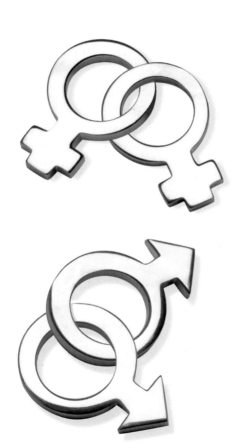

Edinburgh is a great destination for the gay visitor. Much of the scene is centred round the pink triangle between Broughton Street and the top of Leith Walk, each hosting a plethora of venues. Edinburgh in the warm months attracts a multitude of international tourists, so the gay scene is thriving and constantly changing, but in the winter months it can feel like a village. Lots of action happens around the hub of the Blue Moon café and three main bars – Planet Out, The New Town bar and The Laughing Duck. Amazingly CC Blooms is the only club open every night, however, there's a whole series of clubs which become gay on a particular night of the week, and around the weekend there's a bevvy to choose from. Cruising takes place at Calton Hill at night. Warriston Cemetry also attracts cruisers, but be warned, it can be dangerous. During the Festival Edinburgh is like nowhere else on earth. Cruising and international exchanges can happen at all times of day and night, and there's always plenty of films, theatre, dance, music and books of gay interest to devour.

Bars

CC Blooms, 23-24 Greenside Pl, **T** 556 9331. *Daily 2230-0300 (bar from 1800). Free. Map 3, G10, p251* Ever-popular gay bar and club next to the Playhouse Theatre. Upstairs is the bar – lots of mirrors and neon; downstairs is the sweaty dance floor. Packed to the gunnels late at night and weekends.

The Claremont, 133-135 East Claremont St, **T** 556 5662. *Map 3, D9, p251* Quirky, sci-fi bar which has a bear/leather night on the 1st and 3rd Saturday of the month.

Habana, 22 Greenside Pl, **T** 558 1270. *Mon-Sat 1200-0100. Free. Map 3, G10, p251* Next door to CC Blooms, this intimate, trendy bar attracts a pre-clubbing young crowd.

Frenchies, 87-89 Rose St Lane North. **T** 225 7651. *Daily 1300-0100. Free. Map 2, C1, p248* Right in the heart of town is this intimate friendly gay bar, full of regulars.

The Laughing Duck, 24 Howe St, **T** 220 2376. *Mon-Thu 1100-2300, Fri-Sat till 0100, Sun 1130-2300. Map 3, G6, p250* Gay in the 80s, straight in the 90s, and now gay again, this big airy bar attracts a mixed age range. Upstairs lounge, downstairs is a dance floor/function room.

New Town Bar, Dublin St, **T** 538 7775. *Mon-Thu 1200-0100, Fri-Sat 1200-0200, Sun 1230-0100. Map 3, G8, p251* The city's cruisiest male bar. Men of all ages congregate in the basement club at weekends.

Planet Out, Greenside Pl, **T** 524 0061. *Mon-Fri 1600-0100, Sat-Sun 1400-0100. Free. Map 3, G10, p251* Friendly, happy, award-winning gay bar which attracts a loyal following for its various weekly activities including DJs and a quiz. Voted 'Best Pub in Scotland' by NOW UK magazine.

Cafés

Blue Moon Café, 1 Barony St, **T** 557 0911. *Mon-Fri 1100-2330, Sat-Sun 0900-0030. Map 3, G9, p251* The hub of gay Edinburgh, this long café winds over three rooms and is ideal for coffee and chat. Mobbed at weekends, especially round the cosy flame fire in the backroom, it's an ideal meeting place to find out what's happening in the city. Unfortunately the food is poor.

Sala Café Bar, 60 Broughton St, **T** 478 7069. *Daily 1100-2300. Map 3, F9, p251* Opened in March 2003, this exciting two-roomed café bar is connected with the old Lesbian and Gay Centre.

Clubs

Joy, at Ego, Picardy Pl, **T** 478 7434. *2300-0300. Map 3, G9, p251* £8 members; £10 non-members. Every fourth Saturday of the month is the night of Joy. It's house music on the main floor from Edinburgh club veterans Alan and Maggie Joy and Brett King, whereas downstairs is more chart, funk and soul from Trendy Wendy and Sally F.

Velvet, at Ego. *2300-0300.* £6 (£5); two for one before 2330. Monthly night with resident DJ Michelle playing the tunes for lesbians and their specially invited male friends.

Vibe, at Ego. *2300-0300.* £2. Every Tuesday night DJ James Longworth plays the tunes at this lively charty, hands in the air dance party.

Wiggle, at Ego. *2230-0300*. £9. A new monthly night from Maggie and Alan Joy with DJs Trendy Wendy and Jon Pleased keeping it camp in the main room, while Sally F and Michelle spin some R&B, hip hop and indie downstairs. Offering something a little different on a Saturday.

Eye Candy, at Massa, 36-39 Market St, **T** 226 4224. *2300-0300. Map 2, E5, p248* £10 (£8). Dress wild for this weekly Saturday night club with resident DJs creating their infamous glam house party.

Tackno, at Massa. *2300-0300*. £10 (£8). Monthly Sunday night of fun and frolics, chart, soul and funk from the legendary Trendy Wendy.

Luvely, at The Liquid Room, 9c Victoria St, **T** 225 2564. *2230-0300. Map 2, F3, p248* £8 members, £10 non members. A fantastic full-on monthly night of hard house from the resident DJs. Dress up and live it up on a Luvely Saturday.

Taste, at The Liquid Room. *2300-0300*. £5 before 2330, £6 members, £8 non-members after 2330, £10 non-members on guest DJ nights. Sunday is the night for Taste with its heady mix of house and garage from DJs Fisher and Price.

Mingin', at Studio 24 (upstairs), Calton Rd, **T** 558 3758. *2230-0300. Map 2, C10, p249* £5 before 2400, £6 after. DJs Brian Dempster and Alan Joy bring this fortnightly Saturday night billed as a dark, sexy, dirty, house club.

Contacts

Lesbian Line, **T** 557 0751. *Mon-Thu 1930-2200*. Helpline for lesbians wanting to discuss everything from relationships, coming out and sexual health.

LGBT Police Link, LGB Centre, 60 Broughton St, **T** 620 5138. *Mon 1800-1900*. Call if you want a chat with the community officer.

Lothian Gay and Lesbian Switchboard, **T** 556 4049. Daily 1930-2200. Helpline for both lesbians and gay men tackling a variety of issues from health to families.

Scotsgay Magazine, **T** 0845-1208062, www.scotsgay.co.uk Monthly gay magazine with articles and listings of events happening in and around Scotland.

Saunas

Number 18 Sauna, 18 Albert Pl, **T** 553 3222, www.number 18sauna.co.uk *Sun-Fri 1200-2200, Sat 1200-2300. Map 3, E11, p251* £8 (£5). Popular sauna on two levels – cabins, lounge on ground floor, and the basement has a jacuzzi, steam room, sauna and dark room.

Townhouse Sauna, 53 East Claremont St, **T** 556 6116, www.townhouse-sauna.co.uk *Sun-Thu 1200-2300, Sat-Sun 1200-2400. Map 3, E8, p251* £9 (£6). Converted Georgian townhouse on four levels provides luxury sauna/cruising facilities. Special offers throughout the week.

Steamworks, 5 Broughton Market, **T** 477 3567, www.steam works-sauna.co.uk *Daily 1100-2300. Map 3, G8, p251* £5-£10. New in March 2003, round the corner from the Blue Moon Café.

Edinburgh has more than enough to interest even the most demanding of kids – from hyperactive toddlers to monosyllabic adolescents. Most of the sights listed in this section are aimed at younger children, but those approaching teenage years should enjoy the more ghoulish aspects of the city, particularly the Ghost Tours (see p28), Edinburgh Dungeon (see p44) and Sir Jules Thorn Exhibition (see p64), as well as the rather more educational and interactive Museum of Scotland (see p60).

Sadly, eating out with children in the UK can be a frustrating experience and too many establishments are downright unhelpful. Furthermore, the attitude in the UK to breast-feeding in public is still some way behind the rest of Europe. Aside from those places listed in this section, the following restaurants are relatively child-friendly, with high chairs and nappy-changing facilities: Bann UK (p144), City Art Centre (p149), Est Est Est (p153), Café Hub (p149); Lower Aisle (p150); Negociants (p173); Terrace Café (p159) and Valvona & Crolla (p158).

Sights

Deep Sea World, North Queensferry, **T** 0930-100300. *Apr-Oct daily 1000-1800; Jul-Aug 1000-1830; Nov-Mar Mon-Fri 1100-1700, Sat and Sun 1000-1800. Adult £6.25, children £3.95. See also p109* The world's largest underwater viewing tunnel, through which you pass on a moving walkway, coming face-to-face with sharks, conger eels and all manner of strange sea creatures. There is also a display of species from the Amazon rainforest.

Dynamic Earth, Holyrood Rd, **T** 550 7800, www.dynamicearth. co.uk *Apr-Oct daily 1000-1800; Nov-Mar Wed-Sun 1000-1700. Adults £8.45, children £4.95, family (2 adults, 2 kids) £22.50 Map 2, D12, p249 See also p53* It's science, Jim, but not as we know it. Aspires to tell the "story of the planet", with all the requisite state-of-the-art bangs and fizzes.

Edinburgh Zoo, Corstorphine Rd, **T** 334 9171, www.edinburgh zoo.org.uk *Daily Apr-Sep daily 0900-1800; Oct-Mar daily 0900-1630. Adults £7, children £4, OAPs £4.50. Buses 12, 26/26A and 31 from Haymarket and Princes St. Penguin Parade at 1400 daily Mar-Oct, weather permitting. Map 1, p247 See also p94* Kids will love the famous penguin parade and to see them swimming underwater in the world's largest penguin pool.

Museum of Childhood, 42 High St, **T** 529 4142. *Mon-Sat 1000-1700, Sun in Jul-Aug 1200-1700. Free. Map 2, E7, p249 See also p46* Touted as the noisiest museum in the world. It also covers the serious issues of childhood, such as health and education, but that doesn't spoil the fun.

Portobello Beach. *Buses 2, 15, 26, 42, 66, X86 from Princes St. Map 1, p247 See also p102* Long, sandy beach, perfect for

Kids

sandcastle-building on those rare sunny days. Also amusement arcades, funfairs, chips and ice cream to delay the onset of boredom.

Royal Botanic Garden, Inverleith Row, **T** 552 7171. *Daily 1000-1600 Nov-Feb; till 1800 Mar-Apr and Sep-Oct; till 2000 May-Aug. Free. Buses 8, 17, 23 and 27 from the city centre. Map 3, p250 See also p85* Huge open spaces and not a dog poo in sight.

Eating

Harry Ramsden's, Newhaven Harbour, **T** 551 5566. *Sun-Fri 1200-2100; Sat till 2200. No smoking. Map 6, A2, p256* Famous fish and chips emporium. A great place to take the kids.

Umberto's, 2 Bonnington Rd La, **T** 554 1314. *Mon-Sat 1200-1430, 1700-2200, Sun 1200-1800. Map 6, E5, p256* Very good Italian food with a Scottish flavour at probably the most children-friendly restaurant in town.

Luca's, 16 Morningside Rd, **T** 446 0233. *Daily 0900-2130. Map 4, H10, p253* Parents should be arrested if they try to leave town without coming to this temple of ice cream wondrousness.

Facilities and services

Clambers, at the Royal Commonwealth Pool, Dalkeith Rd, **T** 667 7211. Mon-Fri 1000-2000, Sat and Sun 1000-1630. Play centre for children aged 3-10, also suitable for children with special needs.

Babybusters, **T** 337 3421. Babysitting and crèche services for evenings and occasional daytimes.

Banks and ATMs

Bank opening hours are Monday-Friday from 0930 to between 1600 and 1700. Some larger branches may also be open later on Thursdays and on Saturday mornings. You can withdraw cash from selected banks and ATMs (or cashpoints as they are called in Britain) with your credit/debit card. Visa card holders can use the Bank of Scotland, Clydesdale Bank, Royal Bank of Scotland and TSB ATMs; Access/MasterCard holders can use the Royal Bank and Clydesdale; Amex card holders can use the Bank of Scotland.

Bicycle hire

Bike Trax, 7-11 Lochrin Pl, **T** 228 6633, www.biketrax.co.uk *Map 4, E11, p253* £15 for full day, £10 for half day. Very friendly and helpful and will recommend local routes. **Scottish Cycle** Safaris *Map 2, F7, p249* (see Tours, p26). £15 per day.

Car hire

Arnold Clark, Lochrin Pl, Tollcross, **T** 228 4747. **Avis**, 100 Dalry Rd, **T** 337 6363. **Century Car Rental**, 1 Murrayburn Rd, **T** 455 7314. **Condor Self Drive**, 45 Lochrin Pl, **T** 229 6333, sales@condorselfdrive.com **Enterprise Rent-a-Car**, Block B, Unit 15, Sighthill Shopping Centre, **T** 442 4440. **Ford Rent-A-Car**, 12 Annandale St, **T** 557 0000. **Gran Turismo**, 31 Woodburn Terr, **T** 466 3447, www.granturismo.demon.co.uk **Melville's Hire Drive**, 9 Clifton Terr, **T** 337 5333, enquiries@melvilles.co.uk The main companies are also at the airport, see p20.

Dentists

Edinburgh Dental Institute, Level 7, Lauriston Building, Lauriston Pl, **T** 536 4931. *Mon-Fri 0900-1500.* Free walk-in emergency treatment though you still need to book an appointment. If it's not an emergency but you need to see a dentist, look in the Yellow Pages or call the Primary Care department (see under Doctors).

Disabled

Full details of disabled access on public transport from **Traveline**, **T** 0800-232323. For more information, contact **Disability Scotland**, Princes House, 5 Shandwick Pl, EH2 4RG, **T** 229 8632. The **Lothian Coalition for Disabled People**, **T** 475 2360, **F** 475 2392, publishes *Access in Lothian*, which they will send out on request. **Artlink**, 13a Spittal St, EH3 9DY, **T** 229 3555, gives telephone advice on access to arts venues throughout the city and provides an escort service for people with disabilities.

Doctors

If you need to see a doctor look in the Yellow Pages, or call the Primary Care department, **T** 536 9000.

Electricity

The current in Britain is 240V AC. Plugs have three square pins and adapters are widely available.

Embassies and consulates

Australia, 7 George St, **T** 624 3333. **Canada**, 30 Lothian Rd, **T** 220 4333. **France**, 11 Randolph Terr, **T** 225 7954. **Germany**, 16 Eglinton Cres, **T** 337 2323. **Italy**, 32 Melville St, **T** 226 3631. **Netherlands**, 53 George St, **T** 220 3226. **Spain**, 63 North Castle St, **T** 220 3226. **Sweden**, 22 Hanover St, **T** 220 6050. **USA**, 3 Regent Terr, **T** 556 8315.

Emergency numbers

Police, **fire brigade** and **ambulance**, **T** 999. **Rape crisis centre**, **T** 556 9437.

Genealogical research

Scottish Genealogy Society Library & Family History Centre, 15 Victoria Terr, **T** 220 3677. *Tue and Thu 1030-1730, Wed 1030-2030, Sat 1000-1700*. **Scottish Roots Ancestral Research**

Service, 16 Forth St, **T** 477 8214. *Mon-Fri 0900-1700 by appointment.*

Hospitals
Royal Infirmary of Edinburgh, 1 Lauriston Place, **T** 536 1000. Edinburgh's 24-hour walk-in accident and emergency department.

Internet/email
Easy Everything, Hanover Buildings, 58 Rose St, **T** 220 3580. Open 24 hours and the cheapest in town at £1 per hour at peak times. **Web 13**, 13 Bread St, **T** 229 8883. *Mon-Fri 0800-2000, Sat 0800-1800, Sun 1200-1800.* There's also a cybercafé at 98 Victoria St. *Daily 1000-2300.*

Launderettes
Sundial laundrettes offer coin-operated or service washes, full laundry service, ironing, dry cleaning and alterations. They have several branches at: 7 East London St, **T** 556 2743, next to the Lost Sock Diner (see p157); 84 Dalry Rd, **T** 538 7002; and 17 Roseneath St, **T** 229 2137. **Tarvit Laundrette**, 7 Tarvit St, **T** 229 6382.

Left luggage
At the airport and Waverley train station (daily 0700-2300. £4.50 per item for up to 24 hours).

Libraries
Central Library, George IV Bridge, **T** 225 5884. *Mon-Fri 0900-2100, Sat 0900-1300.* Excellent Scottish and local reference sections. **National Library of Scotland**, George IV Bridge, **T** 226 4531, enquiries@nls.uk *Mon-Fri 0930-2030, Sat 0930-1300.* Superb copyright library, for research purposes only. Reference facilities at the Map Room, 33 Salisbury Pl. *Mon-Fri 0930-1700, Sat 0930-1300.*

Lost property

Property found and handed in to the police (including property found in taxis) is sent to the Police HQ at Fettes Av, **T** 311 3131. *Mon-Fri 0900-1700*. There are lost property departments at Edinburgh Airport, **T** 333 1000, and Waverley train station, **T** 550 2711. Lothian Buses have a lost property department at Shrub Place, **T** 554 4494. *Mon-Fri 1000-1330*.

Media

One of the two main 'quality' Scottish dailies is *The Scotsman*, which is based in Edinburgh and is very useful during the Festival. The city's evening paper is the *Evening News*. To find out what's on and where consult *The List*, a lively fortnightly listings magazine telling you everything you need to know about events in Edinburgh and Glasgow. The local commercial radio station is Radio Forth (97.3FM) which is good for traffic reports.

Pharmacies (late night)

Boots, 48 Shandwick Pl, **T** 225 6757. *Mon-Sat 0800-2100, Sun 1000-1700*. In an emergency outside these times go to The Royal Infirmary.

Police

The police information centre is at 188 High St, **T** 226 6966. *Daily 1000-2200*.

Post offices

The central post office is at 8-10 St James Centre. *Mon 0900-1730, Tue-Fri 0830-1730, Sat 0830-1800*. There's also a main office at 7 Hope Street. Other post offices are open Monday-Friday 0900 to 1730 and Saturday 0900 to 1230 or 1300. Smaller sub-post offices are closed for an hour at lunch (1300-1400).

Public holidays
New Year's Day and **2 January**, **Good Friday** and **Easter Monday**, **May Day** (the first Monday in May), **Victoria Day** (the last Monday in May), **Autumn holiday** (mid-September), **25 and 26 December** (Christmas Day and Boxing Day). Banks are closed during these holidays and sights and shops may be affected to varying degrees.

Taxi firms
Capital Castle Taxis, **T** 228 2555. **Central Radio Taxis**, **T** 229 2468. **City Cabs**, **T** 228 1211. **Edinburgh Taxis**, **T** 228 8989. **Radio Cabs**, **T** 225 9000.

Telephone
Most public payphones are operated by British Telecom (BT) and take either coins (10p, 20p, 50p and £1), credit cards or phonecards, which are available at newsagents and post offices displaying the BT logo and come in denominations of £2, £3, £5 and £10. Note that 20p is the minimum charge for a payphone.

Transport enquiries
Lothian Buses, Waverley Bridge Ticket Centre, **T** 554 4494. *Easter-Oct Mon-Sat 0800-1800, Sun 0900-1630; Nov-Easter Tue-Sat 0900-1630.* Also at 27 Hanover St, **T** 555 6363 (enquiries, 24 hours). *Mon-Sat 0830-1800.* Both offices sell travel cards and maps. Waverley Bridge also deals with bus tours. **First Edinburgh**, **T** 663 9233, www.firstedinburgh.co.uk *Mon-Fri 0830-1700.* **Traveline**, 2 Cockburn St, **T** 0800-232323 (local calls), or **T** 225 3858 (national calls). *Mon-Fri 0830-2000.* Public transport information service.

Travel agents
STA Travel, 27 Forrest Rd, **T** 226 7747. **Edinburgh Travel Centre**, 196 Rose St, **T** 226 2019; 92 South Clerk St, **T** 667 9488; and 3 Bristo Square, **T** 668 2221.

A sprint through history

AD 626   Edwin of Northumbria captures the Castle Rock and anglifies its name Dun Eidyn (fortress on the hill slope) to Edinburgh.

1018   Malcolm II defeats Edwin and Edinburgh becomes a Scottish town.

1128   Holyrood Abbey is founded by King David I, son of Malcolm III.

1290   The infant Margaret, Maid of Norway, dies with no obvious heir. With 13 claimants to the throne, the Scots ask Edward I of England to settle the dispute and he duly claims lordship over Scotland.

1292-95   John Balliol is appointed King but turns against Edward and forms the Auld Alliance with France.

1296   Edinburgh Castle is sacked by Edward I. Balliol is taken prisoner.

1306   Robert the Bruce is crowned King of Scotland.

1307   Bruce defeats Edward II at Louden Hill.

1313   Bruce's men seize Edinburgh Castle back from the English after scaling the north face of Castle Rock.

1314   Robert the Bruce defeats the English army at Bannockburn and wrests control of Scotland back from Edward II.

1322   Holyrood Abbey sacked by the English.

1329-1390   Robert the Bruce dies. David II crowned King but dies without producing an heir. Robert II, the first of the Stewart dynasty, is crowned King. He abdicates and his son, Robert III, takes the throne.

1424-37	James I crowned King at Scone but is murdered 13 years later. James II crowned King at age of six.
1450	James II has a wall built around the city to protect against invasion by the English. The Nor Loch is formed by flooding pastures to the north of the Castle.
1460	James II dies in battle. James III is crowned and formally recognizes Edinburgh as the country's capital.
1498	Palace of Holyroodhouse established by James IV.
1513	Scots lose at Flodden and James IV is killed in battle. His heir is only 17 months old. Flodden Wall built around the city to strengthen defences.
1524	James V crowned at Holyrood Abbey.
1542-43	James V dies after defeat by Henry VIII at Solway Moss. So begins the minority of his infant daughter, Mary, Queen of Scots, who is pledged by the Treaty of Greenwich to Henry's son, Edward.
1544	The Scots renege on the deal and a furious Henry begins the "Rough Wooing", sacking Edinburgh and Leith and destroying the Old Town and Castle.
1559-60	Calvinist preacher John Knox becomes minister of the High Kirk of St Giles. The following year Scotland legally becomes a Protestant country.
1561-1587	Mary, Queen of Scots returns from France. She marries Henry, Lord Darnley in 1565 and a year later gives birth to James VI. The same year her secretary, David Rizzio, is brutally murdered at

Holyroodhouse. Darnley is murdered the following year and Mary marries her lover, the Earl of Bothwell. She is imprisoned and forced to abdicate in favour of her son. She escapes and flees to England where Elizabeth I places her under house arrest for 19 years before having her executed.

1583	Edinburgh Univeristy is founded.
1603	Queen Elizabeth I dies. James VI of Scotland also becomes James I of England.
1625	James dies. His son, Charles I, becomes King.
1645	A plague wipes out the city's population.
1649	Following the English Civil War, Charles I is executed. Charles II is chosen as his successor.
1650	The city is taken by Oliver Cromwell.
1660	The Restoration of Charles II to the throne.
1685	Charles II dies. His brother, the Roman Catholic James VII and II takes the throne.
1688-89	James is deposed and Parliament hands control over to the Protestant Mary and her husband, William of Orange. Protestant forces take control of the Castle.
1694-1702	William and Mary die. Their daughter, Anne, becomes Queen of England and Scotland.
1707	The Act of Union gives political and economic control of Scotland to the English Parliament.
1714	Georgian era begins with the crowning of George I.

1744	Honourable Company of Edinburgh Golfers is formed as the world's first ever official golf club.
1745	Prince Charles Edward Stuart occupies the city with his Jacobite forces but cannot take the Castle.
1788	Deacon Brodie is hanged in Edinburgh.
1816	Nelson Monument (Calton Hill) built to commemorate Nelson's victory at Trafalgar.
1822	George IV visits the city. Work begins on the National Monument, later to be known as 'Edinburgh's Disgrace'.
1824	Great Fire of Edinburgh destroys the upper part of the Royal Mile.
1826-29	Burke and Hare begin their murderous career. Three years later they are caught and Burke is hanged while Hare is freed.
1846	Scott Monument is built. Edinburgh to London rail line completed.
1890	Forth Rail Bridge opened.
1947	First Edinburgh Festival takes place.
1964	Forth Road Bridge opened.
1997	Scotland votes for its own devolved government.
1999	The new Scottish Parliament is "reconvened" after a 300 year adjournment.
2002	Part of the Cowgate destroyed in a huge blaze.

Art and architecture

1751-52	The collapse of an Old Town tenement leads to an investigation which reveals that urgent action is required to rehouse people. The Lord Provost, George Drummond, publishes a set of Proposals for the building of an aristocratic suburb north of Nor' Loch.
1759-65	Part of the Nor' Loch is drained for work to begin on North Bridge. The rest is drained to form Princes Street Gardens. A competition to design a New Town plan is won by an unknown 22-year-old architect, James Craig
1767	Building begins on the New Town.
1772	North Bridge opens, after the first attempt collapsed.
1780	The Mound begins to take shape, formed by the dumping of rubbish from the construction of the New Town.
1785-88	The South Bridge is built and opened to traffic.
1840	The building of the New Town is completed.
1892	Sir Patrick Geddes starts a programme to reoccupy the Old Town with University departments. Many old buildings are saved and restored
2002	The RIBA award-winning Dancebase project is opened in the Grassmarket.
2003	The new Scottish Parliament, the most important building in 300 years of Scottish history, is opened at Holyrood, see p52.

Books

Fiction

Banks, Iain, *Complicity* (1994), Abacus. Crime thriller set in the capital. Though not an Edinburgh writer per se, here Banks explores the darkest recesses of the city's soul.

Brookmyre, Christopher, *Boiling a Frog* (2000), Little, Brown. Scotland's foremost political satirist plays it for laughs in this tale of political intrigue and corruption set in the capital. Scatalogical, violent and hilarious in equal measure, Brookmyre is often compared to Carl Hiaasen. His other Edinburgh-set novels include *Country of the Blind* (1997) and *Quite Ugly One Morning* (1996).

Hird, Laura, *Born Free* (2002), Rebel Inc. Bleak and terrifyingly accurate portrayal of life in a dysfunctional family in West Gorgie, one of Edinburgh's grim council estates. Hird's debut, *Nail and other stories* (1999), is a collection of short stories that also explore the more unsavoury aspects of contemporary urban existence.

Rankin, Ian, *Set in Darkness* (2000), Orion. Like the rest of Rankin's Inspector Rebus novels, this paints a stark, honest picture of contemporary Edinburgh through the eyes of a cynical detective straight out of the Philip Marlowe school of hard cops. Rankin is currently the finest exponent of so-called 'Tartan Noir'. His other Rebus novels include *The Falls* (2001), *Black and Blue* (1998) and *Resurrection Men* (2002), and *Beggars Banquet* (2002) is a collection of short stories featuring Rebus.

Spark, Muriel, *The Prime of Miss Jean Brodie* (1965), Penguin. Classic novel which explores the city's Janus face. The eponymous Jean Brodie teaches at a girls' school in the city in the 1930s and is the very model of respectability. She loves art and culture, and instils in her pupils the need to cultivate an air of 'composure'. She could be the stereotyped lady from the still-genteel suburb of Morningside. Yet Brodie also relishes the power she has over her pupils and has an alarming regard for the fascist teachings of Hitler and Mussolini.

Stevenson, Robert Louis, *Dr Jekyll and Mr Hyde* (1886), London: Longmans Green. One of the classics of horror literature, Stevenson describes the city's dual personality, cleverly capturing the contrast between its genteel exterior and hidden seediness. Respectable Dr Jekyll, who turns into a werewolf at night, does not only symbolize Edinburgh, he was modelled on an Edinburgh citizen, Deacon Brodie, a seemingly respectable town councillor by day and a criminal, gambler and womaniser by night.

Welsh, Irvine, *Trainspotting* (1994), Minerva. Welsh's cult novel shone a spotlight on the city's drug-ridden underbelly and spawned an entire generation of gritty, realist writing. After a succession of hit and miss follow ups, Welsh is back to rude health with his latest, *Porno* (2002), a sequel to *Trainspotting*, which sees the return of Renton, Sick Boy, Spud and Begbie.

History and architecture

Daiches, David, *Edinburgh* (1978), Hamish Hamilton. One of the most authoratative guides to the city's history.

McKean, Charles, *Edinburgh An Illustrated Architectural Guide*, RIAS. An excellent, street by street guide to the city's many fine buildings.

Index

Credits

Footprint credits

Text editor: Catherine Charles
Series editor: Rachel Fielding

Production: Jo Morgan, Mark Thomas
In-house cartography: Claire Benison,
Kevin Feeney, Robert Lunn,
Sarah Sorensen
Proof-reading: Stephanie Lambe

Design: Mytton Williams
Maps: Footprint Handbooks Ltd

Photography credits

Front cover: Robert Harding
Inside: Lee Woolcock (p1 statue in
Princes Street Gardens, p5 Balmoral Hotel
clock tower, p31 Ramsay Gardens,
p105 Forth Road Bridge)
Generic images: John Matchett
Back cover: Lee Woolcock (Dynamic Earth
and Salisbury Crags)

Print

Manufactured in Italy by LegoPrint
Pulp from sustainable forests

Publishing information

Footprint Edinburgh
2nd edition
Text and maps © Footprint
Handbooks Ltd June 2003
ISBN 1 903471 67 2
CIP DATA: a catalogue record for this
book is available from the British Library

® Footprint Handbooks and the Footprint
mark are a registered trademark of
Footprint Handbooks Ltd

Published by Footprint Handbooks
6 Riverside Court
Lower Bristol Road
Bath, BA2 3DZ, UK
T +44 (0)1225 469141
F +44 (0)1225 469461
E discover@footprintbooks.com
W www.footprintbooks.com

Distributed in the USA by
Publishers Group West

All rights reserved. No part of this
publication may be reproduced, stored in
a retrieval system, or transmitted, in any
form or by any means, electronic,
mechanical, photocopying recording, or
otherwise without the prior permission
of Footprint Handbooks Ltd.

Every effort has been made to ensure
that the facts in this pocket Handbook
are accurate. However the authors and
publishers cannot accept responsibility
for any loss, injury or inconvenience
sustained by any traveller as a result
of information or advice contained in
this guide.

Ordnance Survey® This product includes
mapping data licensed from Ordnance
Survey® with the permission of the
Controller of Her Majesty's Stationery
Office. © Crown Copyright. All rights
reserved. Licence No. 100027877.

Complete title list

(P) denotes pocket Handbook

Publishing stuff

For a different view…
choose a Footprint

Over 90 Footprint travel guides
Covering more than 145 of the world's most exciting
countries and cities in Latin America, the Caribbean, Africa, Indian
sub-continent, Australasia, North America, Southeast Asia, the
Middle East and Europe.

Discover so much more…
The finest writers. In-depth knowledge. Entertaining and accessible.
Critical restaurant and hotels reviews. Lively descriptions of all the
attractions. Get away from the crowds.

Advertising

The Royal Yacht *Britannia*,
a Five Star Experience in
Edinburgh's historic port of Leith.

*Take the Britannia Tour Bus from Waverley Bridge or
Lothian Buses no.22 from Princes Street. Open daily.*

**Information Line: 0131 555 5566
www.royalyachtbritannia.co.uk**

OCEAN TERMINAL, LEITH, EDINBURGH

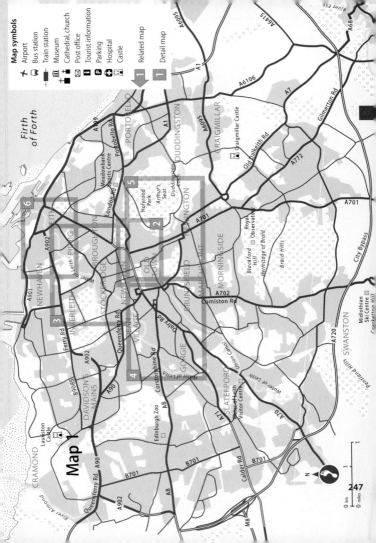

Map 1

Map symbols

✈ Airport
🚌 Bus station
🚆 Train station
🏛 Museum
✝ Cathedral, church
☒ Post office
🛈 Tourist information
🅿 Parking
🏥 Hospital
🏰 Castle

1 Related map

1 Detail map

Firth of Forth

River Esk

River Almond

A68
A6415
A68
River Esk
A6095
A1
A6106
A7
A1
A199
A901
A902
A6095
A701
A772
A701
Gilmerton Rd
Old Dalkeith Rd
City Bypass

CRAMOND
DAVIDSON'S MAINS
NEWHAVEN
LEITH
PORTOBELLO
DUDDINGSTON
CRAIGMILLAR
SWANSTON
MORNINGSIDE
MARCHMONT
BRUNTSFIELD
GORGIE
SLATEFORD
DEAN VILLAGE
INVERLEITH
STOCKBRIDGE
BROUGHTON
LEITH PILRIG
NEW TOWN
OLD TOWN
NEWINGTON

Lauriston Castle
Edinburgh Zoo
Water of Leith Visitor Centre
Union Canal
Water of Leith
Craigmillar Castle
Royal Observatory
Blackford Hill
Hermitage of Braid
Braid Hills
Midlothian Ski Centre
Craigmillar Hill
Pentland Hills
Meadowbank Sports Centre
Holyrood Park
Arthur's Seat
Duddingston Loch

Portobello Rd
London Rd
Ferry Rd
Queensferry Rd
Dalry Rd
Corstorphine Rd
Comiston Rd
Queensferry Rd
Calder Rd

A90
A8
A70
A71
A702
A720
B9085
B701
B701

N

0 km   1
0 miles 1

247

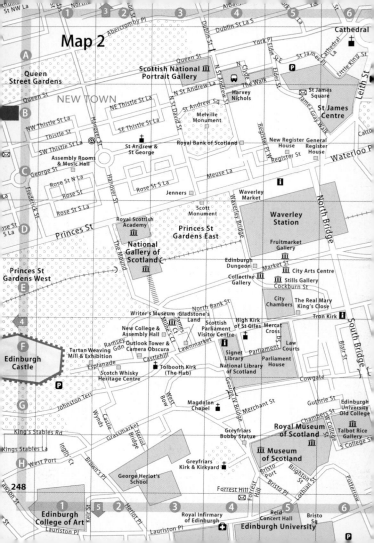

Map 2

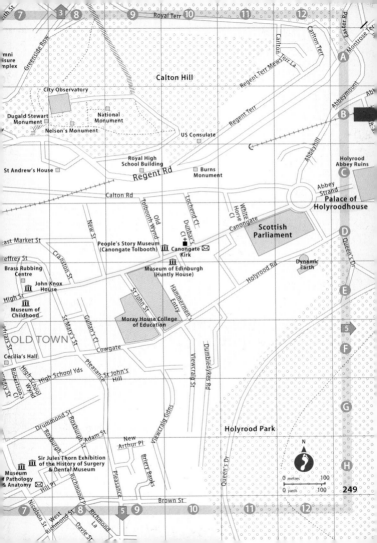

Easter Rd

Montrose Terr

A

Abbeymount

B

Ab

Holyrood
Abbey Ruins

C

Calton Hill

Regent Terr Mews La

Carlton Terr

Carlton Terr

Carlton Terr La

Regent Terr

City Observatory

Dugald Stewart
Monument

National
Monument

Nelson's Monument

US Consulate

Abbeyhill

Abbey
Strand

Palace of
Holyroodhouse

St Andrew's House

Royal High
School Building

Burns
Monument

Regent Rd

Calton Rd

Last Market St

New St

Cranston St

Jeffrey St

Brass Rubbing
Centre

John Knox
House

High St

Museum of
Childhood

OLD TOWN

Tolbooth Wynd

Old Tolbooth Wynd

Dunbar's Cl.

Lochend Cl.

White
Horse
Cl

Canongate

People's Story Museum
(Canongate Tolbooth)

Canongate
Kirk

Museum of Edinburgh
(Huntly House)

St John's St

Hammermen's
Entry

St Mary's Cl.

Gullan's Cl.

Moray House College
of Education

Cowgate

Scottish
Parliament

Holyrood Rd

Dynamic
Earth

D

Queen's Dr

E

5

F

Cecilia's Hall

High School Yds

High St Wynd

Robertson's Cl.

Mary's Cl.

St Mary's Cl.

Pleasance

St John's
Hill

Viewcraig St

Dumbiedykes Rd

G

Drummond St

Roxburgh St

Adam St

New
Arthur Pl

Briery Banks

Viewcraig Gdns

Queen's Dr

Holyrood Park

Sir Jules Thorn Exhibition
of the History of Surgery &
Dental Museum

Museum of
Pathology
& Anatomy

Hill Pl

N

0 metres   100

0 yards   100

H

249

Nicolson St

West
Richmond St

Richmond
La

Davie St

Pleasance

Richmond Pl

Brown St

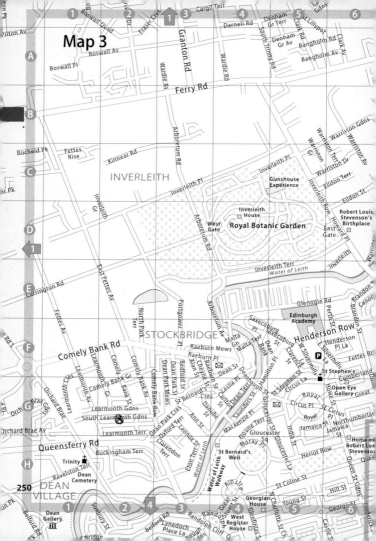

Map 3

A
B
C
D
E
F
G
H

Pilton Av
Boswall Quad
Fraser Cres
Cargill Terr
Darnell Rd
Denham Gr Terr
St Lillypot
Gdns

Boswall Av
Boswall Pl
Granton Rd
South Trinity Rd
Denham Gr Av
Bangholm Rd
Clark Rd
Bangholm Av

Wardie Av
Ferry Rd
Wardie Rd

Rocheid Pk
Fettes Rise
Kinnear Rd
Arboretum Rd
Inverleith Pl
Glasshouse Experience
Warriston Gdns
Warriston Terr
Warriston Gr
Warriston Dr
Warriston Av
Eildon Terr
Eildon St

er Pk
INVERLEITH
Inverleith Gr
Inverleith Pl
Inverleith Row
Howard Pl
Robert Louis Stevenson's Birthplace

Inverleith House
West Gate
Royal Botanic Garden
East Gate

Carrington Rd
East Fettes Av
Arboretum Pl
Inverleith Terr
Water of Leith
Warri

Fettes Av
North Park Terr
Portgower Pl
Arboretum Av
Glenogle Rd
Perth St
Brandon Terr
Brandon

Comely Bank Rd
STOCKBRIDGE
Saxe-Coburg Pl
Saxe-Coburg St
Edinburgh Academy
W Silvermills La
Henderson Row
Henderson Pl La
Fettes Rc

Learmonth Cres
Learmonth Gr
Comely Bank Av
Comely Bank Pl
Raeburn Mews
Raeburn Pl
Malta Terr
Malta Grn
Dean Bank
Silvermills
Henderson Pl
St Stephen's

Comely Bank St
Bedford St
Dean St
Leslie Pl
Hamilton Pl
St Stephen St
Circus La
Cumberland
Open Eye Gallery
Great

Learmonth Gdns
Dean Park Mews
St Bernard's Cres
Carlton St
Danube St
Deanhaugh St
Saunders St
Kerr St
St Stephen St
Royal Circus
Royal Circus Pl
SE Circus
Jamaica St
Northumberla
Jamaica

South Learmonth Gdns
Dean Park Cres
Oxford Terr
Ann St
Mackenzie Pl
Doune Terr
India St
Gloucester La
Home of Robert Lo Stevenson

Learmonth Terr
Clarendon Cres
Eton Terr
Lennox St
Water of Leith
Gloucester Pl
Gloucester St
Moray Pl
Heriot Row

Queensferry Rd
Buckingham Terr
St Bernard's Well
Georgian House
HILL ST

Orchard Brae
Trinity
Ravelston Terr
Dean Cemetery
Water of Leith Walkway
Ainslie Pl
St Colme St
Young St

250
DEAN VILLAGE
Sunbury St
Belford Rd
Randolph Cliff
Randolph Cres
West Register House
Great Stuart St
N Charlotte St
Charlotte Sq
George

Dean Gallery
Lynedoch Place La
Randolph Cliff
Bridge

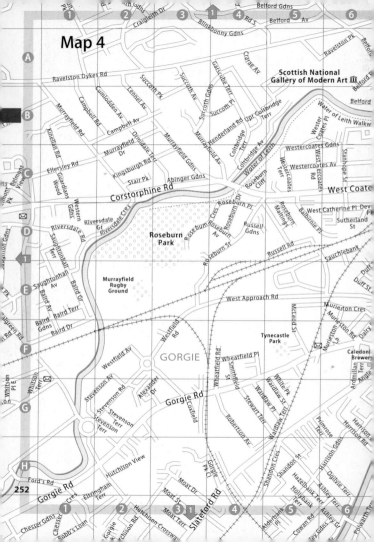

Map 4

Scottish National
Gallery of Modern Art

West Coate

Roseburn
Park

Murrayfield
Rugby
Ground

West Approach Rd

Tynecastle
Park

Caledoni
Brewery

GORGIE

Gorgie Rd

Gorgie Rd

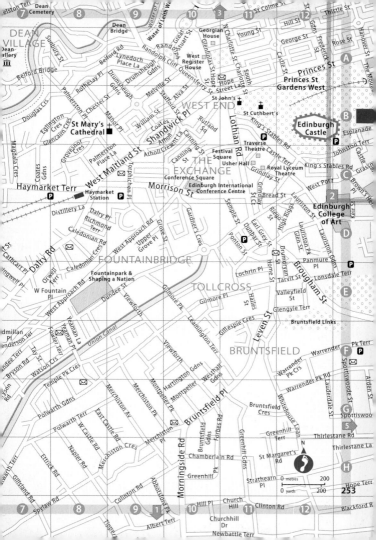

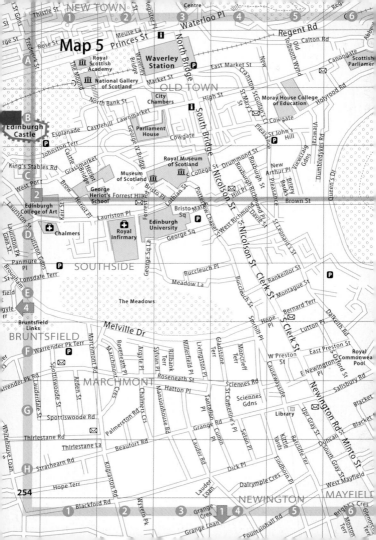